Pebbles

Pebbles
Michael Rosen

Smokestack Books
School Farm
Nether Silton
Thirsk
North Yorkshire YO7 2JZ
e-mail: info@smokestack-books.co.uk
www.smokestack-books.co.uk

ISBN 9781739473440

Cover photo:
Emma-Louise Williams

Smokestack Books
is represented by
Inpress Ltd

For Emma

Introduction

I'm interested in a paradox about thought: on the one hand it appears to be continuous and yet it seems to happen in short bursts. In one day, hundreds, perhaps thousands of short bursts. It feels impossible to capture them all. No point in trying. But what if I could grab the sensation of how the thoughts happen? I decided to use Twitter (now X) to do this because there's a limit there in the size of message you can post. This seemed to match the fragmentary feeling of sensations, happenings, reveries and, on occasions, more logical thoughts.

One day, my wife Emma and I were on a beach and she took the photo you see on the cover: me asleep surrounded by pebbles. Earlier, I had been playing with them, piling them up, dropping them, gazing at them stretching away into the distance. I caught myself wondering about how we talk of a 'beach' as a single entity but it's made up of millions of grains of sand or in this case, pebbles. When Emma showed me the photo, I had an immediate sense that it was an image of what I was trying to do with the fragments of thought, the tweet-poems. Each one could be picked up and looked at but together they made something else.

I hope that people will read this book doing what I did with the pebbles – looking at single stones but running them together to make something whole.

This puts the book into a different tradition from the poetry book that creates profundity on every page - and a great tradition that is too. Instead, it's trying to grab the randomness, the everydayness mixed in with what at the next moment might be some kind of insight. I hope by my saying this, you'll experiment with the book yourself, running the poems on from page to page letting them knock against each other, letting the meaning you make of one, drift into the meaning of the next.

In schools, I talk of poems having 'secret strings', invisible lines of cohesion between words, sounds and images. In this book, the secret strings are between poems rather than running within them.

And, as I say, to school students and teachers, if you find a secret string, it's a secret string; you don't have to worry about whether the writer put it there. If this sounds as if I am against coherence, let me say, it's just the opposite. I'm very much in favour of the coherence that you make.

Michael Rosen
April 2024

Shhh, he said,
don't let anyone know,
but the damage in me
means I'm not afraid
of anything else.
You can throw anything at me
rocks, acid, rage,
drive over me if you like,
it just won't matter
because it won't matter as much
as the damage.
The damage looks after me.
Shhh.

There were whole days
when all I thought about
was the number of steps
I did yesterday
and the number of steps
I might do later today.
I kept saying:
'Creeps in this petty pace from day to day'
that's me.

The end of the garlic pickle.
The last of the pickle.
No more pickle.
Just smears in the pickle jar
where the pickle once was.

Interesting:
all year round
people believe
what doctors and nurses
tell them,
and then
when those same doctors and nurses
want to be paid properly,
people say they're not telling the truth.

Spring is here:
the first outdoor nail-cut of the year.
Ants – you're in for a treat:
a keratin feast.
You don't see that on *Masterchef*.

This morning's big challenge:
how to eat blackberries
without getting pips
stuck in my teeth.
I think it's important
at my stage in life
to take on the big stuff,
the things that really matter.

Grief is being sorry
that things aren't the way
they were.
But nothing is the way it was.
Even in grief
we have to see
we are part of all things
becoming different.

What is not done
will have to stay not done.
These things won't run off.
The night will hold them
till the morning.

Water running over fingers
they're not expert at stopping or keeping.
They love the feeling
of the running and twisting.
They like to let the water go.
Tomorrow
I'll make a cup.
Palms at the bottom
fingers for the sides.
That'll work.
but I bet they won't
love the feeling.

There was a fight on a station
The reason for the fight was that
some people
were trying to stop someone
getting on the train.
They succeeded.
The train left without him.
The court heard
that even though the train had gone
they went on trying to stop him
from getting on the train.

A plumber came
to unblock the sinks.
He talked of
drains breaking
walls subsiding.
Nothing could be done.
He left.
Another plumber came
He had a hoover.
There was a roar.
He cleared it.
But what was 'it'?
We dream of giant plugs of fat
speckled with coffee grounds.

A man came and unblocked the sink.
Kkkkcccchhhhckkkkgggggggllllllkkkgllllllll

There's something
I should be doing
and I'm not doing it.
It doesn't even matter
anymore
what it is
I'm not doing.
All that's going on
is a person not doing
what they should be doing.

I shouldn't let myself feel smug
that the overnight soak of the pans
worked.
A brisk scrub this morning
did it.
Just that.
I shouldn't let myself feel smug
about it.

I lost my suitcase.
It wasn't in the loft.
It wasn't in the cupboard
under the stairs
It wasn't in the wardrobe
in the bedroom.

It was in a suitcase.
The suitcase
was in a suitcase.
It was the suitcase's joke.

When my brother was 16
and I was 12,
he told me
 that the square root of minus 1
is 'i'.
Luckily we had a lot of other things in common
so this didn't ruin our relationship.

Hey do you remember
those Maths problems
about calculating the height of the pyramids
but we never had to calculate
how many people died building them?

Don't overdo the pumpernickel.
One slice is enough.
You may get away with two slices.
Any more is plain unwise.
Listen and learn.

I've got documents
from the archives of Vichy France:
impeccable ledgers
full of carefully worked out percentages
of how much to take from Jews
as part of 'Aryanisation'
prior to them
(including my father's uncle)
being deported to Auschwitz.
Maths without ethics.

Maths problem for Rishi Sunak:

How many students
have to run away
for there to be enough Maths teachers
to teach compulsory Maths
to all 16–18 year-olds?

Hey do you remember
those Maths problems
about 'men' digging holes
and if you got fewer men to dig the hole,
how long would it take?
Note we were never asked
why we were being asked a question
about making fewer men
work harder.
Maths without ethics.

Inflation?
The government's got it covered:
dampen demand.
How to dampen demand?
Simples: freeze wages.
Poor people can't afford to buy
what they need
because prices are too high.
Solution: make them poorer.
Maths without ethics.

Yesterday, at the Good Grief podcast
we were asked
what did we learn
from the death of a loved one.
I thought it was that
we are all part of life on earth
where we are all in the midst of
bacteria, viruses, machines,
storms, earthquakes, decay,
or a moment's error
and we resist these things
for some of the time,
never all of the time,
and for different lengths of time.

One of the nicest things
I ever did with Eddie
about a year or so
before he died was
see Dylan Moran
at the Edinburgh Festival.
It's a great memory
of doing something together
and laughing and laughing and laughing.

I find things in my back
buried beneath the surface
small crustaceans I think
fossils possibly
who sat in the skin
waiting for this moment
to emerge
be noticed
and then vanish.
How many years
have they waited in there
only for it to be all over
in a second?

Just as I was walking to the supermarket
this morning
thinking that my brain has holes in it
through which names escape.
I disturbed
two birds
who complained
that I didn't know
whether they were sparrows
or chaffinches.

A doctor once told me
that when Eddie died
he wouldn't have known anything about it:
he was asleep
and the antigens
from the meningitis bacterium in his blood
eroded the membranes around his cells
so his body inside turned to mush.

More than 20 years later
a doctor said to me in hospital
'Will you sign a piece of paper to let us
put you to sleep?'
I said, 'Will I wake up?'
He said 'You've got a 50:50 chance.'

I thought, if I don't wake up
it won't matter because
I won't know anything about it.
Like Eddie.

I signed.

I did an audition for *Masterchef*.
I made poppadom ice cream.
Didn't get the gig.
I was the lead actor
in the play of my life
called My Life
but I discovered later
there was another version
called Life
in which
I am an extra.

A travel firm has just asked me:
"Enjoyed your journey?
We won't be happy unless we know you were truly happy with
your recent journey."
I've replied:
"Before I answer your questions,
Travel firm,
can we talk about your life?
You sound unhappy.
Do you want to talk about your feelings?
What kind of place are you in right now?"

Every day
someone tightens up my hamstrings.
I remember a bow-saw
in my father's tool box,
where he twisted a peg
between two threads of cord
to tighten the bow.
Someone sticks that peg
into my hamstrings every day
and it twists them tight.

St George's Day
I was just going about being scaly
and breathing fire
when a guy turned up
and speared me.
I've heard since
that they made him a saint.
Be fair.
It was a double act.
I was the fall guy.
Ernie helped Eric get the laughs.
Maybe I'm not worth a sainthood.
OK.
But something. Surely.

Someone please save Kafka
from the hands of Raab
(who claimed the Report on him was
'Kafkaesque') .

The Trial and other books
are about powerless, low-status people
facing the cruelty of the state,
not a high-status person
like him
facing due process,
open to scrutiny.

We did the Witches' song from Macbeth
but I didn't know it was going to be in St David's Church.
They filled the pews from the back to the front
and mid-way through the 'wool of bat and toe of frog'
I was a preacher of 'hell-broth boil and bubble'
and they were all cooling it with 'a baboon's blood'.

A teacher brought
some children
to my poetry workshop
today.
She was well prepared.
She was wearing high viz
and carrying something
with a label on it.
It said:
Eagle Sick Bucket.

I went back to where
I used to play
70 years ago.
The ground was just as stony.
The same gravel.
I picked up a pebble.
I've kept it.
It's in my coat pocket.
I put my hand
into my pocket
and pass the pebble
between my fingers.

A woman
just stopped me
from stepping out
into the traffic.
I didn't know her.
She said,
'I didn't want you to die again.'

Monday is the week's begun day
Tuesday is blues day
Wednesday is friends day
Thursday is the cat purrs day
Friday is try day
Saturday is make it matter day
Sunday is the week's done day

When I give my old
(very old)
phone
too much to do,
it gets hot.
It's as if it's trying too hard
to do too much
too quickly.
Maybe it's not just
that it gets hot.
More like it's getting
hot and bothered.

Does it matter
that I'm confused
as to whether Eddie died
in the middle of the night
early in the morning
of today April 26,
or that he died
late at night of
today April 26?
It was night.
That's what I'm certain about.

The doorbell stopped working.
People pressed it,
but no one got up
and went to the door.
Someone came to mend the doorbell.
He got it to work
and tested it by pressing it
again and again.
No one got up
and went to the door.

This is to inform you
that you will be appearing
at our venue
next month.
We informed you earlier
that you would be appearing
at our venue
next month.
This is to inform you
that you won't be appearing
at our venue
next month.

I am a father
I am a child
I watch the children I have
I watch the child I was.
If I listen to what's in my head
the child I was teaches me.
if I listen to my children
they teach me too.
I am a child
I am a father.

Ikh bin a tate
Ikh bin a kind
Ikh kuk oyf di kinder vos ikh hob
ikh kuk oyf di kind vos ikh bin geven
Oyb ikh hern tsu vos iz in mayn kop,
der kind in mir, lernt mir.
Oyb ikh hern mayne kinder
zey lernen mir oykh.
ikh bin a kind.
ikh bin a tate.
(Yiddish)

Es iz geven an alter kaker fun Vin
Vos iz geven nokh in mitndrin,
Er hot gegloybt latkes
Zaynen geven zayne gatkes
Un itst zogt nisht aher nisht ahin
(Yiddish limerick)

There was an old geezer from Vienna
who was in quite a lot of bother.
He thought that *latkes* (potato fritters)
were his *gatkes* (long johns/trousers)
and now he says 'Neither there nor here'.

Every day I walk past a place called
Beauty Academy.
I guess they do beauty courses
in there.
It's an Academy
so why not?
Beauty Academy.
Sounds lovely.
I often wonder
if I went in there
and did one of their courses
I would become beautiful.
So far
I haven't enrolled.

I heard an account
on radio
of the situation in Sudan,
described as war lords
whose only purpose
in being in power
is to enrich themselves.
Thank goodness
we in the West
don't live in societies
run like that.

A scratching in the cupboard!
I opened the door.
It was a mouse.
The cat was there.
The mouse looked at the cat.
The cat looked at the mouse.
I thought this could go on forever.
I picked up the mouse.
I lobbed it at the cat.
The cat caught it
and said, 'What a great mouser, I am.'

I do like these burnt seeds
from off the top of this loaf.
There are some that have
fallen on to the bread board.
The seeds are nutty and chewy.
Or...
are they mouse shit?

Oh ho ho ho
this Welsh thing is oh ho ho ho
it's not as if England has been next to Wales
for quite a long time
so every time we see a Welsh word
we have to say, how strange
how difficult, how odd,
how...
impossible.
oh ho ho ho ho.

There were two girls
in my class at school
who often used to say
to their Jewish friend
that they wished
they were Jewish
but without having to convert.
Those of us who were Jewish
tried to figure out
how that could be done.
We didn't ever figure that
though.

This morning
I am mostly dealing with people
who think I am a cartoonist.
In Art lessons
I tried to be an impressionist.
But not an impressionist painter.
I was doing impressions of teachers.
I didn't do any impressionist painting
I didn't do any painting at all
And none since.

At the new checkout machines
at the supermarket
they tell you not to
put the shopping in your trolley.
You've got to pile it up
on a tray on the side.
If you buy enough shopping
to fill a trolley
there isn't room for it
on the tray.
I put a pot of hummus
in my armpit instead.

There's a bird in the bushes outside
with a machine gun.
Not the usual kind.
It's a bird-sized one.
A small but perfectly formed
Gatling.
Come to think of it
Gatling could be the name of a bird.

Here's my recipe for hummus sauce:
Take one large spoonful of hummus.
Or two large spoonfuls of hummus.
Or three large spoonfuls of hummus.
Add water.
Stir.
Pour on anything.
But especially falafel and salad.
Drink the dribbles left in the jug.
Make smacking noise with lips.

I went to school
with a kid called Alan Fresco.
Al Fresco.
The teachers got fed up with him
because he would never come inside
at the end of playtime.

When I am too awake to be asleep
and too asleep to be awake
I make myself as still as a stone
to see if I have more sleep in me.
Nothing must move.
I focus on one of the flashes
under my eyelid:
a fragment of zebra skin
or a fading traffic light.
It feels like
practising dying.

My daughter Elsie said to me,
'You're an optimistic nihilist.'
'Am I?' I said.
'You don't think there's any point
to existence
but you think that's a good reason
to make the most of it.'
I thought: good that Elsie went to university –
she comes home and tells me stuff
like that.

The train departure board on the platform
was blank.
There was no announcement.
The train came in.
There was still no announcement.
I wondered where the train was going.
I got on
hoping it might go to France
or Canada or Atlantis.
It was going to High Barnet.

We know the word
schadenfreude
is clever at telling us
about a pleasure
we shouldn't really have.
Is there one
in stories and movies
when we enjoy
someone being bad:
pleasure in others' wickedness
knowing that
we won't get the blame?

After 25 years
the memories are as vivid
but the grief isn't as great.

I heard a noise
coming from the kitchen.
I hoped
that it wasn't one of those things
that I wouldn't be able to solve myself:
a leaking tap, a broken fridge.
It was a hot cross bun
saying, Eat me.
I was able to deal with that myself.

The announcement said
if I saw anything that didn't look right
I should call the Transport Police.
I rang them and said,
I've seen stuff that doesn't look right:
sewage in the sea,
Number 10 lockdown parties
Dominic Raab's resignation letter,
and...
but they interrupted me
and said I had the wrong number.

Someone is drawing a straight line
from north to south
across London
imagining a deep rapid transit
underground line
which will start running trains
in 20 years' time
and they will sit in a room
and decide that
it'll be called the
Charles Line.

Final score:
Arsenal 3 Chelsea 1.
Chelsea won the second half (0-1).
That's a fact.
But is it the truth?

It's just occurred to me that
when I was a boy
and radio or TV
liked to parade old, wise, great people
like:
FR Leavis, JB Priestley
or the Dame Ediths:
Evans and Sitwell,
many of them had spent at least
some of their childhoods
in the Victorian era.
Not long ago then.

We note
your safety campaign slogan,
'See it. Say it. Sorted.'
includes a capital 'S' on 'Sorted',
with a full stop after the word,
implying that it's a sentence.
It's not.
Sentences MUST include a finite verb.
A past participle on its own
is NOT SATISFACTORY.

Sentence Police

You Don't Know What You Need
Till They Tell You That You've Got To Have It
Even If You've Never Heard Of It Before
(No 143)

'Bonding Oil: dramatically
increases shine, softness,
and color vibrancy
while minimizing flyaways and frizz.'

Dear Harbor Freight
Thanks for the 170 Piece Stanley Tool Set Offer
newly arrived in my email inbox.
I don't think I'll be taking you up on this
just now
as I can't think of how or why
I'd use 170 tools.
170?
10 max.
That leaves 160
unloved, sad tools.
And that would be wrong.

I wrote to the universe for its views on
life, death, spaghetti bolognese
and tooth ache.
No reply.
Nothing.

He's on his last legs.
He doesn't remember his first legs.
He thinks last legs must be ultimate legs.
He remembers his penultimate legs.
He thinks his legs have lasted quite well.
Those are my last legs? he says.
What are my next legs going to be like?

The state imposes a new rule.
This draws in 100s of people
sneering at people
who don't understand the rule,
can't make the rule work for them,
or who just give up.
It's a bottle
full of fizzy contempt for others
being uncorked.

I visited my old school today
to talk to yr 13s
and I swam in the pool
that's been filled in
ate a school dinner
in the demolished dinners block,
acted in Twelfth Night
on a stage that isn't there,
and talked to Andy
who was in the sixth form
when he died in a car crash

The 'Stop' button on the bus
does not mean 'This is a bus stop'.
does not mean, 'Stop what you're doing.'
How do I know that it means,
'Press me,
and the driver will hear a bell
and will stop the bus at the next
bus stop'?
Such a lot of information
in one word.

I brought an elephant home.
Emma said that I'd never get it through the door.
I said, 'I think I will.'
She was right.
It didn't fit.
'What are we going to do?' I said.
'I'll leave that to you,' she said.
The elephant stood there for a while
then it lay down.

It was the elephant in the room.

When I think of my grandfather
(who I knew as Zeyde)
I think of Hackney
and a ground floor flat
with chickens in the backyard.
Since I've found out
where his parents came from
I've come to realise
that his childhood
must have been
full of their memories of
Kovno in Lithuania.

Every time I buy the Offspring
his dough balls
I think of Colonel Bogey.

What overwhelms us
is not death
but grief.
Death is biology.
Grief is mind.

We are numb
we are not aware of heat
and shoe size.
We are incurious.
We don't notice nails
and the cutting of nails.
We forget
how we were.
We don't ask questions.
It's all now, now.
Your thoughts about us
don't reach us.
If they did,
it wouldn't matter.
We don't care.

One of us was
locked in a room.
He said it changed his life.
Another one of us
was told he was a coward.
He said that it
locked him in the prison house
of language
and that this changed his life.

Until I started shopping
at the deli on the corner
I thought there were bagels
with either sesame seeds
or onions,
(alongside other bagels too, of course).
But this deli
produces a bagel:
with both sesame seeds
and onions.
The hybrid bagel.
I had no idea this was even
possible.

This evening in Yiddish class
we learnt:
'*Men ken nisht tantsn*
af tsvey khasenes
mit eyn tukhes.
It means:
'You can't dance
at two weddings
with one bum'.

I was reading an American book
and I couldn't work out if
the character was
agin or agin.
Or both.
Some of us are.

Whichever way
Steve in Truckee, California and I
do our DNA tests
we don't come up as cousins.
This proves
my grandfather was mistaken
that he had what his sister-in-law called
'an illegitimate child'.
So was the child's mother muddled?
Or was she hoping he'd help out?

Our French teacher was Mrs Hill.
She was French.
She said she was
Madame 'eel'.
She wore black high heels
black hair piled on to her head
ringlets down the side of her face
painted nails
tight skirt.
We had French names.
I was Michel.
'Michel!' she said.
I liked French a lot.

At the Eye Clinic just now,
the reading test
didn't go well.
I got stuck.
The nurse said
No, try again,
So I ad-libbed
Z? Q?
She said, Blink!
It was worse:
M?
No.
I tried numbers:
7? 8?
No good.
I tried Yiddish letters:
Alef? Vov?
No good.
It felt like Maths lessons,
1958.

What is it?
I don't know.
Why don't you know?
It was an elusive allusive illusion delusion.

My train is not stopping
at my stop
because there are graffiti
on the side,
the guard says.
Good to know
the power of writing.

There's a hole
in the armpit of my jumper.
I figure that
if I don't raise my right arm
too high
no one will notice.
I must remember
not to wear it
tomorrow
when I visit a school
and sing
(with actions)
'we can't go over it'.

It started with
you could do

then it was
you should do

then it was
you shouldn't do

then it was
look what you made me do

then it was
look what you shouldn't have made me do.

then it was
over.

A lot of people say
it's a journey.
All sorts of things can be
a journey.
In fact,
there are so many people in the world
on a journey
that no one's at home.

After Covid
the docs lasered my eyes,
inserted drains
swapped my lenses
for plastic ones;
I dose my eyes up
morning and night
with stuff called things like
bimatoprost timolol
so my eyes were pleased
they got good marks
at the Eye Clinic today.

In Tottenham today
there were so many roads closed off
that you couldn't go anywhere
and you couldn't get back
but if you tried to stop trying
going or coming
and instead,
stopping where you were
there were parking attendants
telling you to move on.

I told the children today
that I got Covid
and as a result
I can't see very well with my left ear
and I can't hear very well with my left eye.
They said, You got that wrong, Michael Rosen.
But then if you think about it
no one can see very well with their left ear
or hear very well with their left eye.

I told the children that I was so ill that they put me to sleep.
They put me to sleep for 40 days and 40 nights,
a bit like the length of time that Noah was in the rain.
Noah was with his wife, I said.
What was Noah's wife called? I asked.
A child said, 'Stephanie.'

I said are there any questions?
One boy said, I've got a question, Michael Rosen.
What's your question? I said,
Do you know my Dad's name?
No, I said.
It's Patrick, he said.

Today
I will be restoring my spirits
by taking the waters
at Tunbridge Wells.
Actually, I won't
because you can't.
You can visit
but not drink.
Says so in the Guide.
I was just getting ready to go to
Tunbridge Wells
and I thought I'd have
a Jane Austen moment.
Done that now.

The police say
that they thought
a woman was a protestor
so they arrested her.
Presumably they thought
she looked like one –
which raises the question,
what does a person
who isn't a protestor
have to look like
to look like a protestor?

They make exams and tests
harder
to make sure
that fewer children do well.
When the results come out
the papers will say that
standards are going down,
which is teachers' fault
and children are becoming stupid.
In an election year
the govt can say
they'll make it all better.

A measure of what is the very best
in this country's education system
is to note that its very top
has produced
Boris Johnson, Liz Truss and Suella Braverman
for whom we are truly thankful.

What greater indictment of
the exam system
is hearing people who
sailed through
the exam system
saying that they can't think of an alternative to
the exam system.

Before my show
people ask me if
I have a presentation.
I say,
'Cher was once asked why she had spent
a million dollars on her body.
She said, "This is all I got, honey."
Same with me,' I say.
I point at my saggy jumper
and what it disguises,
and say
'This is all I got, honey.'

In the mornings
I put my good ear side
deep into the pillow
leaving my fogged ear exposed
and let the muffled moves
of wheelie bins outside
softened creaking door hinges
and complaining cats
drift me back to sleep.

Alastair Campbell says
that the only people
who go on about the dodgy dossier
are journalists.
It's a good point.
None of the dead people in Iraq
ever say anything about it.

They say that primary school
SATs tests
that children have to sit
are not testing children.
They are testing schools.
Is it ethical for one group of people
to be tested
in order to test the worth or ability
of another group?
It's a bit like
whether it's appropriate
to punish one person
for a crime
that someone else has committed.

My favourite defence
of all govt misdemeanours, crimes,
dishonesty, illegal wars, etc
is 'I didn't do it knowingly'
or 'I didn't do it deliberately'.
Or, I acted 'in good faith.'
Kids take note.
If you're hauled up for anything,
just say,
'Yeah but I didn't do it knowingly.'
Or, let's say, you beat someone up,
say,
'I beat him up in good faith.'

There was an empty seat
in front of me at Arsenal today.
In the second half
a guy sat on it.
The guy sitting next to
the empty seat said,
'You can't sit there.'
The guy said, 'I can.'
They started snarling and wrestling.
A steward took them out
and they missed
the rest of the game.

Judging Eurovision
from your sofa
is not about choosing
who you think is best.
It's about
who you think
others will think is the best.
It's like you have to know
the musical tastes
of millions of people.
If you get it right
you win Eurovision.
I say this because
last night
I won Eurovision.

When I was 11
I saw a photo
of my mother holding a baby.
My father said his name was Alan,
a brother who my mother never spoke of.
There was no grave,
no pictures other than this one
no candle to mark his time.
And now the photo has gone too.

In the cupboard
there is a bowl of flying saucers.
They are leftover sweets
from Halloween.
Unwanted treats.
Not wanted then.
Not wanted since.
There must be a reason
why I or someone else –
anyone –
hasn't thrown them away,
but for the moment
I don't know
what that reason is.

Comfort is an important thing
to mention these days.
We encourage people to
get out of their comfort zone.
And we offer them a comfort break.
I'm worried that I'm being told that
I can't have a comfort break
in my comfort zone.
The thing is
my comfort break
is a comfort zone.

In a loaf of sliced bread
is the crust ever a slice
or is it always the crust?
Is a thumb a finger?
It is when I say I have five fingers.
It's not when I say it's a thumb.
A foot doesn't have a thumb.
So the big toe is always a toe.

My father made a box.
He put in it the letters
he sent from Germany
to my mother.
When I was a child
the place for the box
was the cupboard
at the top of the stairs.
My father moved house
three times.
One day
I noticed the box was empty.
The letters had gone.
I've got the box.

A man in a cafe today
told me about his
atrial regurgitation.
He said they'd clipped his mitral valves.
An image came into my mind
from my flunked medical course
of tiny flaps
with fine strings
that seemed to have been put there
by an engineer.

We talked about eating hearts
and I asked him
if he had ever seen the strings.
He said no.
We both reckoned
we hadn't eaten one for years
though I was thinking about
chicken livers
in 'gehakte leber'
(chopped liver)
which isn't much to do with
hearts
or atrial regurgitation.

I've always thought that
Nietzche is niche.

A man on the train says,
'Are you better?'
Am I better than yesterday?
Ah but he's thinking,
am I better than when I was ill?
But then when I was ill
I was unconscious
with a tube down my throat.
I'm not unconscious
with a tube down my throat now.
I'm standing on a train.

I had a few minutes
to talk about
why it's important
for under-5s to talk.
I think how under-5s grow.
How do their minds grow?
How do they find out about
love, hunger, fun.
How do they figure
gravity or winter.
Talking – and singing
will help their minds
do that, I say.

Praise be to Ann Widdecombe.
She says, don't have cheese
in your sandwiches
if you can't afford cheese.
Today I told a hungry man
on the street
to eat a cheese sandwich
with no cheese in it.
Imagine the cheese, I said.
Think Wensleydale,
think Gruyère,
think toasted halloumi.
Who needs cheese
when you've got imagination?
And it's so much healthier.

How do you know
what other people think
unless you hear other people
saying what they think?
How do you know
what you know
unless you say it
and you hear yourself
saying it
or if you hear
other people saying
what they think
of what you said?

The man in the cafe
waved towards his wife and said
'We wear padded pants.'
'Do you?' I said.
'They're different though' he said,
'hers are different from mine.'
I said, 'Yes, they would be.'
'Yes,' he said.
I thought with so much that
people disagree about these days
it was good to agree about something.

'Do you have fruit tea?'

The answer wasn't yes or no.
It was:
'We've stopped doing fruit tea.'

So now I feel good.
I feel really glad
that there were loads of people
before me
who could get fruit tea
and I can't.

My cousin has sent me a screenshot
of a letter from my father aged about 6
writing to his Ma in hospital.
'I hope you soon be out'
with 50 kisses on the bottom.
It doesn't say
he was worried
she wouldn't ever be out
or
that his father hadn't come from America
and never would.

As I was a medic
in my 1st week
I had to buy a skull.
I put it on the mantlepiece in the room
that I shared with Dave
from Sunderland.
He told me that
he watched Sunderland play.
Guys throw meat pies at you
and the pies hit you on your head,
he said.
Or on your skull,
I thought.

Why did they think that
mind and body
are two different things?
Apart from anything else
you can see that
they're joined together.

My barber says today
he's going to be in a film
about Modigliani
with Al Pacino.
I say, when my dad was 10
he met Modigliani's model,
Beatrice Hastings
in Belsize Park.
Are you going to play Modigliani?
I say.
No, he says.
Can you do my eyebrows? I say.
Sure, he says.

The things you don't know
that go on in your body.
I see that saddle pulmonary embolism
is a rare type of acute pulmonary embolism
that can lead to sudden hemodynamic collapse
and death.
I had one of them.

A child
A book
A read
A chat.
This is the way the mind grows.
Not with a test
but a tale.

I had to learn how to walk again.
My grown-up sons come over
and take the Dad for a walk.
I don't have a lead.
I don't run off.
And I don't sniff other Dads.

I've just been through Runcorn.
That's twice in two days.
Last time it was in the other direction.
Life can be quite exciting at times.
I certainly wasn't expecting it to be
as exciting as this though.

I was in the basement
and thought
there used to be a fireplace here.
What's holding up
the three chimney breasts in the rooms above?
Alan said there must be something.
in there.
He cut a hole in the ceiling
put his hand in
and said, 'No. There's nothing,
apart from two 9-inch nails.'

Jim Rose of the famous Rose Report
on reading in primary schools
invited me into see him.
He had a copy of *Bear Hunt.*
He said:
'I've put the alphabetic principle in place.
I want to know, Michael,
how do I make this book come alive?'
I started singing the words with the actions.
'Yes,' he said, 'but how do we get that done
all over the country?'

When did we start reaching out?
We used to be in touch.
I'm just getting in touch to say that
I've climbed Everest.
Now we do less touching
and more reaching.
When that gets to sound a bit stale
maybe we could stretch.
I'm just stretching out to tell you
I've made a cake.

The woman in the chemist says
'Have you got any piles cream?'
'Yes,' says the chemist.
'I've heard that if you put piles cream on
under your eyes,' she says,
'it gets rid of your wrinkles.
But maybe you just end up
looking like an arsehole.'

She bought the cream.

Important conversation at the checkout.
Woman who ensures that I'm old enough
to buy wine says that Arsenal failed
for mental reasons.
I say it's physical.
I wonder though,
if we're not being holistic enough.
Why separate mind and body?
I was old enough to buy wine.

The best invites I get
are for events that took place
several days before
the invite was sent to me.
I always feel
that I should make the effort
to be there.

I love it
that you can read a tweet
and if you react to it,
with a 'like',
you get a message saying,
'Sorry! this tweet has been deleted'.
But has it though?
What was it you just read?
What is something you can see
but is deleted?
It's there.
But not there.

Every day
I wonder where are
the words and thoughts
I had right after the induced coma?
I watch film of the Doc saying to me
'Michael, you've got children!'
I say, 'Apparently.'
Nurses have written in my 'Patient Diary'
that I talk about wanting to go home.
None of it is there.

Thing and process.
Different, we say.
But don't we only notice
and know
it's a thing
because we learn and know
the process it's in?
What really is the difference
between a felt tip
and a highlighter pen?

The person who goes to bed
wearing socks
will find
that there are some mornings
when one sock is on
and the other sock is off.
This would be of no consequence
were it not for the fact
that it is impossible
to find the missing sock.

Here is a chunk of knowledge.
These are its parts.
Learn it part by part.
But what if knowing the parts
doesn't explain how it works?
And what if there are other parts
that are essential for explaining
how the thing works
but weren't a part
that we learnt?

The reason why we put
children on separate tables
according to ability
is so that when we test them
we find out
if we've put them
on the right tables.

Tests test what you're supposed to know.
To find out if you do know this
you do pretend tests.
This is how
you learn how to think
in the way that tests
want you to think.
The more pretend tests you do
the more likely it is
you will think
in the way tests
want you to think.

If I say a wall is bricks
this leaves out that
the wall is built.
Bricks is a pile of bricks.
If I say language is words
this leaves out that
language
is built.
Words is a pile of words.

I told my children
when they were small
that Caffé Nero
was Caffé Nerd.
I said
if you go in there and you're a Nerd
they give you free coffee.
I didn't ever succeed
in getting them to believe me.

I was at the shoe shop today
and the person fitting me
was really rude
about the inside of my shoes.
So insolent.

We have two words: conscious and unconscious.
Twice in my life,
I've been in a state
when everyone thought I was conscious
but I have no memory
and have never had a memory
of these periods of time.
One was twelve hours long.
One was five days long or more.
What is this time?
Where is it?

Teenage boys spot me on the bus.
They shout, 'It's the meme guy!'
It's because I say 'Nice!' on a video.
Americans think
I say 'Noice!'
and have written NOICE
on the meme as a subtitle.
In China though
I am 'Nice granpa'.
Apparently.
In Mandarin:
Nice ye-ye.

Nice.

I asked the cats
whether it's an hour since
I've taken my thyroxine pills
so that I can have breakfast.
No answer.
Typical.
After all I do for them
and they can't even do me a little favour
like that.

The whole point of the rhetoric
round immigration
is that it has nothing to do with
whether people are
or are not
migrating,
and everything to do with
encouraging people
to be afraid of strangers.

There are times in life
when we have to face
a sad truth:
like when you realise
that you haven't left yourself
enough leftovers
from last night's takeaway curry.

You can tell
when your children
have grown-up:
they tell you
of a hummus
that is better
than the one you usually buy.

Hey old Bumblebee!
No need to bumble about.
You know the way you came in?
That's the way to go out.

Ted Hughes
said that he wanted to write about
the crowiness of crows.
Now that we've heard
on the News that
Cadbury's Flakes have become
too flaky
to go into the ice cream
of a 99
we need to look at
the flakiness of flakes.

Another story on Boris Johnson's jollies
during Lockdowns.
If I'd died during the 1st Lockdown
my family wouldn't have been able to see me.
This'd be sad
but if Lockdowns slowed down transmission
it'd be good.
But then if so,
Johnson's jollies
could have speeded up transmission.

If you miss out on your
usual Friday night takeaway
it is essential that
you get one as soon as possible
following that Friday.
On no account
wait till the next Friday
even if it means
having a takeaway
on a Thursday
and then again as usual
on the Friday.

On the menu
it said that the dessert
had 'parline' with it.
'Excuse me,'
I said to the waitress
'what is 'parline'?.
Or is it 'parlin-ay?' I said
figuring that it might be Italian
and I could use my incredible ability
to pronounce Italian words.
'It's praline,' she said.

I have just received an email from a
'manufactory'.
They say,
'Are you troubled about the aesthetic surface of your parts?'

After my talk
about Covid:
the look of loss
in a man's face
as he tells me of
a weakness
in every part of his body.
The look of loss
in a woman's face
as she tells me of
a heart that
suddenly pumps
at a rate
that leaves her
weak and breathless.

You said Leonard Cohen
I said Bob Dylan
You said Paul Simon
I said Allen Ginsberg
They said, Do you want to be king?
I said, king of what?
Just king, they said, will you sign?
I signed everything
apart from
Do you agree to be a Catholic?

I thought I'd go beyond.
Go to a new level.
High risk.
A fresh and special way to eat hummus.
A treat:
Fig and spelt sourdough crackers.
Brittle, smoky
underneath the smear.
Then I cut my tongue.
That'll teach me.

Pictures of Eddie and me
have gone up on the new Arsenal mural:
Eddie is on my left next to
the green dinosaur, Gunnersaurus.
Thank you, Arsenal.

Printers are like the kid in school
who looks for a moment
like he's going to do
what you ask him to do
but in actual fact he doesn't.
Then when he does get round
to doing a bit of homework,
he eats it.

They're talking on the radio about
tasering the over 90-year-olds.

If I last that long,
that's something for me to look forward to.

I've just been for my Covid booster jab
at the Chemist.
I wasn't sure there was room for him and me
in the cubicle.
I offered to sit outside
but he said no
that wouldn't work.

Woman gets on the bus:
'Do you go to Finsbury Park?'
'Yes', says the driver.
He waits for her to use her card.
'No', she says,
'I'm travelling tomorrow.'
And gets off the bus.

Ever since I did a DNA test,
every morning I wake up
and there's news in my email inbox of
someone who is the son of my 4th cousin.
The thing is
it's always someone different.
I now know
that I have a hell of a lot of
sons of 4th cousins.

There is no cover up
We are not covering up
It is wrong to suggest there is a cover up
Nothing has been covered up
There is nothing to cover up
If there was something to cover up
we wouldn't cover it up
but there is nothing to cover up
and we're not making a fuss about this.

Dear Cabinet Office
Our lives were in your hands.
Whatever you're hiding was a matter of life and death to us.
Some of us were lucky to survive.
Many did not.
We're entitled to know why.
Every little bit of it.
Michael Rosen

Since my tracheostomy hole
wouldn't close up
I've got to know hypergranulation.
In the land of hypergranulation
wounds take days to heal.
You nick your finger
on a take-away curry box
and it still hurts
when you have your next curry
a week later.
Warning:
don't bite your tongue.

There is no evidence
We can't find the evidence
If there was evidence
it wouldn't be important evidence.
The fact that we can't find the evidence
is not evidence.
We think you have the evidence.
We think that when you look at the evidence
you'll find that it isn't evidence.

We have nothing to hide.
We haven't hidden anything.
There wasn't anything to hide anyway.
If there had been something to hide
we wouldn't have hidden it.
We have only hidden nothing.
Whenever we saw nothing, we hid it.
But we didn't find anything.
Or nothing.

Because we have seen
that there is nothing to see
you can't see it.
We think
it would be dangerous
if people did see something
because that would mean
in the future
people would want to see
something.
That's why we're saying
there's nothing to see.

The Ancient Chinese writers showed us
that we don't have to say that we are sad
that time is passing
or that death happens.
We can say instead
if we want to
that a leaf on a tree in autumn
falls on to a river
and the river takes it
out to sea.

I wrote a poem called
'Don't Drown'.
It's about some things
you can do
to avoid drowning.
I tell young people
that it's not about
avoiding drowning
and it's not about
drowning.

Welcome to UK, Martian.
We do things brilliantly.
When things go wrong
we have an inquiry.
It can inquire into anything
including the government.
Though if the government
thinks there are things
that it shouldn't inquire into
then the inquiry
can't inquire into them.
Welcome.

That moment of heaven
when I was a student
and I discovered a tin of
Patak's Curry in a Hurry.

I thought feeling dizzy
was feeling dizzy
until I discovered labyrinthitis.
My last spell of labyrinthitis
lasted five days.
I have slain the minotaur.

Sometimes
the only sensible explanation
is that
we're eating each other.

It was a delight to be at your festival
of culture and politics.
And such a warm occasion.
Thanks very much for inviting me
to give a talk about the NHS, recovery and death.
My next book is called 'I am Wriggly'.
Not sure it'll run to an hour though.

Wierd looks wierd
Weird looks weirder.

The hole in my neck
from the tracheostomy
didn't close
because I hypergranulated.
'Cosmetics' cauterised it with
silver nitrate.
The hole closed.
I cut my tongue on Monday.
I'm hypergranulating.
I'm imagining silver nitrate on it.
Now
I'll try to stop imagining that.

I think it's a very good idea
that we have a free speech tsar.
Tsars were very well known
for their love of free speech
especially in Siberia.

Today
I walked into a glass door.
I saw a sign
and walked towards it.
The only problem
was that there was a door
between me
and the sign.
I quickly looked around
to see who was to blame.
There was no one.
That proved
it was the door's fault.

Now that the govt is opposing its own inquiry
and given that the Mail said
that some members of the judiciary were
'enemies of the people',
perhaps a next step for the government
should be to take legal action against the judiciary.
(Emoji needed here for something eating itself.)

After the govt had set up
a govt inquiry,
the govt said that
the inquiry could not inquire
into the govt.
In that case
would it not be easier
for the govt
to dissolve the inquiry
and inquire into the possibility
of having another inquiry?

(after Bertolt Brecht)

My Covid booster jab
was in my right arm.
I ask myself
why does my left arm
think that my Covid booster jab
was in my left arm?

Found on the BBC website:

The health secretary told the Commons
work had started at two London hospitals

The trust that manages the hospitals
says it is not aware of the work

You sent me an email asking me if I had sent an email.
I sent you an email saying that
I had sent an email and asked you if you had got it.
You said that you had got the email
in which I asked you: if you had got the email,
was that the email I meant?
I sent an email asking you
whether you would answer that question.
You didn't reply to that email.

A kookaburra is outside our house.
Right now.
Sorry.
No.
A bloke walked past
and thought something was
funny.
As you were.

Skip-wrestling:
a sport involving trucks with grabs
lifting and dropping skips
in streets.
Marks awarded according to:
number of skips being wrestled
in one skip-wrestling session,
height from which skip is dropped.
loudness of yelling of skip-guys.
earliness in morning.

People are fascinated (not)
by my story of hyper-granulation.
Since Covid,
any wound 'granulates':
the lacerated skin proliferates 'granules'
preventing the wound from closing.
Thus there was a prob
with my trachy 'hole' -
but now a bitten tongue.

News: it's taken a week,
but it's healed!

News in:
an exciting advance has been made
in how society can cure its ills
and make major advances,
even faster and greater than AI.
It's called Fuk-U.
The basic principle behind Fuk-U
is that it's directed at anyone
being non-productive.
This way, we become more productive.

Maybe
there's an idea
in selling words
printed on to little metal plates
that you can tie to your hair.
I'd call them 'fringe magnets'.

In 1945,
people had experienced the depression and war.
In those times,
they had helped each other,
worked together,
saved each other,
seen some loved ones die
for reasons that seemed avoidable.
They chose a govt
that would see
that we should be more
all for one, one for all.

And we can think of it like this:
at some stage in our lives
we are all disabled,
some of us for one second,
some of us for one day,
some of us for one week,
some of us for one month,
some for one year,
some for one decade,
some for several decades,
some for a whole life.

They're cutting the grass at the deserted station,
the station that's been deserted for fifty years or more.
Who's cutting the grass at the deserted station?
Why are they cutting the grass at the deserted station?
What does the deserted station think about that?

Other people got ill
and he had to pay for it out of his taxes.
He said,
'That makes me sick.'
In fact, it made him so sick,
he had to go to the doctors.
which others had paid for.

I tripped up on the way
into the station
and landed face down
by the ticket barriers.
I have found out that
the best medication for dealing with this
is a cinnamon bun.

I've just met the nutritionist
who said to me in hospital
3 years ago,
'What would you like to drink?'
I said, 'An ice-cold smoothie.'
She went away
and came back with a grey bottle
of warm sick.
It was called something like
CureU.
I told her that I haven't forgiven her.

I am named after the man
who coined the phrase
'the unreliable narrator'.
He is Wayne C. Booth,
close friend of my father
in the US Army.
My middle name is Wayne.
I am one of the oldest English-born
Waynes in existence.
Have I narrated this story
reliably?

Just after the coma
I couldn't be relied on
to tell the truth to myself.
The nurse is wearing a medieval knight's
full face visor, I said to myself.
I asked another nurse
Why is she wearing a medieval knight's visor?
She isn't, she said
I was the unreliable narrator of myself.

quartermaster's stores
a pocket full of rye
nine bright shiners
sweet chariot
we'll do the hailing
pop goes the weasel
for all the saints who from their labour rest
curds and whey
the bosom of Abraham
singing and singing it
not knowing
what they were
and it didn't matter

The afterlife is here.
I remember him.
You remember him.
People I don't know
remember him.
The afterlife is here.

When I was at university
I shared a flat with two guys.
We had very different tastes in music.
Mike loved Dylan's *John Wesley Harding*.
Don loved Dylan's *Just Like Tom Thumb's Blues*
I loved Dylan's *Hard Rain's Gonna Fall*.
Shared living is difficult.

Someone asks
did we survive the whole term?
I reply
We did.
And over the next 50 years
Don's love of *Just Like Tom Thumb's Blues*
has finally hit me.
I'm converted.
The 850,000 views of one of the YouTube versions
are all mine.

The recorder is dead
or nearly dead
we hear
so people are posting
their recorder achievements:
'I can play the first six notes
of *Silent Night*' etc.
Up till now
I haven't revealed
that I can 'bend notes'
on a harmonica
or 'blues harp'
as we north London
blues players call it.

Paddington Station.
Time for breakfast.
Sushi?
I don't think so.

New book signing technique today:
I signed for about an hour
while eating lunch.
The lunch included
a pile of raw onion
which I ate with my fingers
as I didn't have a fork.
Each book will now
taste of onion.

Sometimes
when I was about ten
and my dad and I
were doing some bit of DIY
like sanding down an old cupboard
he'd say:
'Were it not better done, as others use,
To sport with Amaryllis in the shade?'
I'd say
'I don't know.'
And we'd get on with
the sanding.

O dear.
My train being held up.
Standstill.
Apparently
'there's a Cross Country Service ahead of us that is experiencing problems'.
When I was at school
we used to run cross country
on Harrow Weald Common
and I used to experience problems too.

Every day
I like to set myself a challenge.
It's mostly the same challenge:
will I be able to sneeze
silently?
The silent sneeze
begins where all sneezes start
but defiant and resolute
work of nose, mouth
and fingers
keeps the sneeze
as no more than
a noiseless spasm.

After the coma
I was in a geriatric ward.
Some of the agency night nurses
seemed irritated.
One wouldn't let me have the buzzer.
One got cross
when I fell out of bed.
I was lonely and called home.
Emma couldn't come in.
At least you, Boris
were having parties though.
That's good.

Here is a lesson
in how to not take responsibility
for your own actions:
'I am now being forced out of Parliament...'
Actually... er... no, you've resigned.

The automatic checkout
at the supermarket
knows a lot:
after I'd shown it the bar code
on the hummus pot
it knew whether I'd put the hummus
on the tray
or not.
Tonight
I asked it if it knew
who won the Champions League Final.
It did not.

Now that my youngest offspring
has finished at secondary school
he can't go on banning me
from accepting their invitations.

Report back from French A-level.
Offspring says it was OK.
One more exam to go.
Then that's the last of offsprings
through school.
I've been a non-stop school parent and step-parent
for 44 years.
(Something in my eye...)

For parents of children sitting the Phonics Screening Check:
it's not a reading test.
It tests whether children
can say a short word
that they see in a list of words.
A list of words is not a piece of writing.
Meanwhile,
I hope you enjoy sharing books with your children.

In our Yiddish class,
when we get stuck on a word
that we can't read,
our teacher asks us to read on
and see if we can come back
and read it.
This is known as 'multi-cueing'.
Young children doing systematic synthetic phonics
are in theory not supposed to do that.
It's discouraged.

Every night
we hear a sound
from the restaurant out the back of us
like a hundred or perhaps five hundred
bottles falling into a bin.
I see a waterfall of bottles.
They sound angry.
On the way down
they don't want to break
but nothing can stop them
so they smash.
All of them.

When the pest control man came
he said he'd get rid of the wasp nest
by feeding poisoned water into the nest.
The drones would take it into the queen
and it would kill her off
but what is it with you people?
If it wasn't for wasps
you'd be surrounded with
heaps of dead stuff.

I love it when the news says
'people close to Boris Johnson'.
Love the image.
People sitting or standing close to Boris Johnson.
Really near.
Some of them touching.
Like arms.
Or legs.
I say it slowly:
'people
close
to
Boris
Johnson'.

If someone dies of Covid, there are people who say,
they didn't die of Covid.
If someone gets very ill from Covid, there are people who say
they're not ill from Covid.
If someone gets mildly ill from Covid, there are people who say,
'There, I told you, Covid is just like having a cold.'

Do people who believe Covid
was a hoax,
believe that their doctor is hoaxing them
about other stuff too?
Or is it just Covid
that doctors have been hoaxing them about?
Do they go to the doctor and say,
'OK, you hoaxed me about Covid,
but can you give me something for my earache?'

I don't know where everything is
all the time.
I don't know where everything is
some of the time.
I do know where some things are
all of the time.
I do know where some other things are
some of the time.
Some of the time I don't know
where some things are.

I once met a bloke
who marched up and down
in his bed-sit
playing a whistle with one hand
and a small drum with the other.
The drum hung from a hook
on the end of the whistle.
I've never seen one since.
Maybe I've been looking
in the wrong places.

I don't know why or how
but I once found myself
sitting in the back of a car
with Glenda Jackson.
She was an MP by then
but I did want to say
that she was very good
in *Women in Love*
but I stopped myself.
She was very good though.

The routine is clear:
show the bar code to the machine,
place the item on the tray.
When all items have been shown
and placed, pay.
You're now free
to load your trolley.
Why then
do I set off alarms
by loading the items in my trolley
before I pay?
Am I a bandit?

Last night:
after the dal
and gobi bhaji
a bowl of
cold
chopped
strawberries.

At school
at Easter
I wondered
if anyone in my family
was one of those Pharisees.
I hoped not.
And did the other kids
wonder
if I was one?

Anonymous tweeters
raging in the twilight
demanding replies
giving out orders
flinging insults
summoning enemies
to an imaginary court
calling for sympathy
signposting injustice
spotting conspiracies
claiming expertise
staying anonymous

There were two 'menswear' shops
in Pinner
when I was growing up.
One was called John Booth.
The other, Harry Reed.
My mother would say to me,
'You look a complete 'shlump'
in that jacket.
Why don't you get a new one
from that Harry Boothroyd's?
He does nice jackets.'

I met someone
I was at primary school with,
who was in the sixth form
with Reg Dwight.
She said,
'We used to say,
"Ah, look at little Reg on the piano.
He's doing well, isn't he?"'

He talks of people being on
'borrowed time'.
What does this mean?
Who does 'on borrowed time' apply to?
People over 70, 80, 90?
When do we hit this category:
'borrowed time'?
Who or what do we 'borrow' it from?
We live, we die.
Does he look at some people and say,
they're borrowing time?

Me and you,
we're up to our eyes in debt.
We are sooooooooo borrowing time.
I go to the time-bank every day,
and get out a few more hours.
I've got a time-bank card.
Bang the wall.
Another 20 minutes.
Or are we massively overdrawn
the moment we're born
and life is just a long haul
trying to pay it back?

I sometimes feel
that as I'm someone
who just got through,
I can or should speak
for those who didn't.
I guess the bereaved
can speak about bereavement
and what they saw.
I guess I'm trying to speak
about dying.

Father sang:
'Auf de' schwäb'sche Eisebahne
Gibt's gar viele Haltstatione:
Schtuagart Ulm and Biberach'
Found it online
for the first time just now!
Last line's been in my head as
'Shtur gadurum an beeber ow'
for 70 years!

Was asked to turn in
a couple of
choop
lip smack
NOICE!
performances
for two dudes
on Crouch Hill Station
today.
Was happy to oblige.

I get up and read how I wasn't ill
or
the test that said I got Covid wasn't Covid
or
it was a cold
or
it was flu
or
the people who died would have died anyway
or
all the doctors and nurses were in on the hoax
or
they were dancing not working
or
it was a plan
to sell me drugs

I was in a cab
and the driver said
he was moving out of the area.
He couldn't stand it anymore.
It's full of foreigners, he said.
Where are you moving to? I said.
Spain, he said.

Someone tells me
I fell for the scam.
The Covid scam.
I suppose
that's why I got blood clots
in my pulmonary artery.
And why I got bleeds in my brain
which have knocked out
most of the sight from my left eye
and most of the hearing from my left ear.
That's how scams work.
One moment you're fine
then the next
you get fooled
and all of a sudden
blam
you can't see out of one eye.

How is it
even possible
that sometimes
I manage
to bite
the underside
of
my tongue?

A bloke on Twitter (anonymous)
has been spending time
diagnosing what I got
in 2020.
He sits at his keyboard
coming up with diagnoses:
it was flu, he says,
it was the vaccine, he says.
I'm torn.
Shall I believe him
or shall I believe
the professor consultant
who diagnosed me
at the time?

At the edge of the park
there was a place you could eat
that my mother called the British Restaurant.
She took me there
and I had meat, cabbage, carrots
and gravy,
apple pie and custard.
If I think now about
the look on my mother's face
I think we ate there
for political reasons

In the corner of our local park
there was a hut, nettles and brambles
where an old man
lived with a pig.
When we got bored of kicking
a ball around
we would push through the nettles
and stare at him
and the pig.
He stared at us
and then he'd say,
'Clear off out of it.'

One of us
found a manhole cover in the park.
We lifted it up
and there was a ladder.
We went down
and there were beds
with blankets,
old tins
and ciggy packets.
We said we'd come back
and make it our den.
We did go back
but it was cemented over.

By the time I was 11
we reckoned we knew every derelict shed
and back alley
every wall you could bunk over
every stream you could wade in
every pond you could pond in.
On Facebook
people put up pictures
of tunnels, caves in chalk mines
under where we lived
that we never knew.

One of the chalk mines
runs under our old school.
A bloke who lived in a folly
nearby
used to dig the chalk out
secretly and sell it.
A few years ago
the playground fell in
and they found the tunnels
and caves
he had made.

Re my earlier posts about the pig-man,
the air-raid shelter and the British Restaurant,
I just found this online:
'During World War II the grounds of West House
were used for Civil Defence purposes
with a trench air raid shelter,
a British Restaurant built in the park
and piggeries set up.'

Platform 0
on Kings Cross Station.
I like looking at
Platform 0
on Kings Cross Station.
When Jean-Paul Sartre
wrote about
Being and Nothingness
I'm guessing
he was thinking about
Platform 0
on Kings Cross Station.

A man on Twitter says it was flu.
I write back:
You don't know if I had flu or not.
You weren't doing my blood tests,
MRI scans,
CT scans,
temperature checks,
SAT checks
Covid tests.
You're also anonymous,
so you can say what you want.
He says, how do you know it wasn't a vaccine side effect?
I say, good point but this was March 2020.
There were no Covid vaccinations.

He has more than 78,062 followers.

One of my father's uncles fought for France in WW1.
One fought for Germany.
After the war
one was the best man
at the other's wedding.
Vichy France handed one over to the Nazis.
The Nazis arrested the other.
They were both killed in Auschwitz.

A man writes to me on Twitter:
'You didn't have Covid
because it doesn't exist.'
To prove it he puts up a picture of a man
standing in his living room
saying Covid doesn't exist.
I write back saying
This changes everything.
A bloke standing in his living room,
saying stuff.

I'm convinced.

I think I'm on a train
going south to Morden.
The announcer says
I'm on a train
going north to High Barnet.
I check the stations:
yes
I am on a train
going south to Morden.
The announcer
carries on telling me
I'm on a train
going north to High Barnet.

Once
the most important thing
was the deficit
and pay had to be 'capped'.
Now the most important
thing
is inflation
but the remedy is the same:
pay has to be 'capped'.
I don't think
we're supposed to notice
that there are some people
not in view
gaining advantage from all this.

The school I visited today
had a Raymond Carver poem
on the wall in the toilet.
I love Raymond Carver's poems.
The poem in the toilet was called Happiness.
I was happy then.

I was standing in Reception
of a school today
when the Caretaker came up to me and said,
'Are you the plumber?'

Today I told 100s of school students
about how the Nazis killed
my father's uncles and aunt
because they were Jews.
I read them my poems about it.
I talked about refugees.
We wrote a huge group poem together.

I think I shrunk today.
I must have been very small.
On stations
and in streets
people walked into me
and some even stood on me.
I knew there was no point
in complaining
because I was so small
they wouldn't have heard me.

Three years ago today,
I was lying in bed
wondering if,
in the morning,
I'll be able to walk from the ambulance
to our front door
without using Sticky McStickstick
(my NHS stick).

Pre-existing health conditions?
you ask.
Yes I was 74 years-old.
I've checked this
with wise people on Twitter:
and it would have been OK if I'd died
and better that I should die
rather than someone younger
(as if there really is a Mr Death
who comes round
and gives us a choice).

You seem to imagine
that there are people
in this world
who have no
'pre-existing health conditions'
and others who do.
Life is
a pre-existing health condition.
Our bodies are invaded
by bacteria and viruses
and we react.
Sometimes it's the end.
Sometimes it isn't.

When I write
how I nearly died
yes I'm trying to say
this is what happened to me
but I'm also trying to say
this is what happened
to everyone else who nearly died
and everyone else who did die
but who can't speak
and can't say
what the doctors told them
and what it felt like.

Three years ago today
I came home.
My family
put up bunting over the stairs
that spelled
WELCOME
I didn't know
that I'd been away for
three months.

Richard writes:
I have nearly died twice (one occasion technically I did) – get over yourself. It is life's destination with no certainty where, when or how so you should cling to every moment as precious not look to the past.
Only when you accept death can you truly embrace life.

I reply:
Thanks Richard.
I've accepted the death of my son.
I accept my own death every day
all the more so
because just before I was put into
an induced coma for 40 days
I was told that I had a 50:50 chance
of waking up.

The guy on the train said he was an epileptic,
the police had trodden on his phone,
he liked the red meat
they give you in Indian restaurants
which we agreed is called Tandoori,
he played the Vodaphone message
again and again on speakerphone
that said he had run out of money.

The guy on the right in the photo
is called Jez.
Today, Jez taught me how to
stretch my iliotibial band.
In fact
the picture shows someone
(me)
who has just stretched both his
iliotibial bands.

I love it when anonymous tweeters
with minute numbers of followers
tell me that the doctors and nurses
who saved my life
got it wrong.

About ten years ago
a boy stopped me in the street
and said,
'You're fingy, innit?'
I said, 'Yes.'
He said, 'I thought so.'

Laputa is a flying island
in *Gulliver's Travels*
home of the king of Balnibarbi
and used by him to enforce
his rule over the lands below.
Strange that a
Pizza Delivery guy
on the Broadway today
yelled 'Laputa!'angrily
at a driver who cut him up.
I must be missing something
here.

That thing
where shopkeepers
put what you bought into a paperbag,
held the two top corners of the bag
between the fingers of both hands
and spun the bag round
till it was sealed
with two paper knots.
At home
when no one was looking
I practised doing it.

My granddaughter
could live to the 22nd century.
Her grandfather (me)
used to see Bertrand Russell speak
in Trafalgar Square.
Bertrand Russell's grandfather
met Napoleon.

If you listen to Radio 4
don't turn the radio off
when you leave the room.
Today,
I was walking in and out
of where the radio is.
I created a view of the world
made up of
why someone likes ABBA
the latest news from Ukraine
and how a guy can grow
bigger cauliflowers.

I have just broken the world record
for lifetime consumption of chick peas,
whether whole (as in channa dishes)
or pulverised as in falafel and hummus.
This is unverifiable.

My father
growing up in the 1920s
in a two-up, two-down
with his sister, mother, grandparents
and his mother's sisters and brother
had grand ideas, he told me.
He would buy a bar of Rowntrees Milk Motoring
and see himself sitting in an open seater
as the countryside swished past.

Four Trebor Chews for a penny.
If you couldn't afford a penny
you could get three Trebor Chews
for three farthings.

It was hot yesterday
but I always try to leave time
for questions at the end of my shows
or when I'm signing books.
One child told me his name.
I signed his book.
He said,
'Can I ask you a question?'
I said, 'Yes.'
He said,
'Why are you wearing a jumper?'

I was asked tonight
why I am being given the PEN Award.
I said, 'I don't know,
I wasn't one of the judges.'

I've always worked to the rule
Don't scratch your armpits in public.
I don't remember
anyone telling me this.
I don't think my parents
or any teachers said to me:
Don't scratch your armpits in public.
I stick to it, though.
It means that
in private
I give them a right going over

They said today
the under-5s playcentre
is falling apart,
the floors in the corners
are unsafe
no one can afford to repair it,
not the owners
not the council
so it'll be closed.
Imagine a time
when we wouldn't be able to afford
not having an under-5s playcentre.

I met a woman today
who said she was one of the physiotherapists
in my ward
before I went to the Rehab Hospital.
I didn't recognise her
because my brain has wiped
most of that time.
She said that they tried to get me to stand up
and they flopped me over
a double-decker zimmer.

Today
I found myself doing two shows
for audiences that were aged
between 0 and 4.
In fact,
quite a few were 0.
Not all 0 year-olds
are fascinated
by what I've got to say.

Tonight, at the talk
a woman came up at the end
and said that she liked my books
and gave me a present.
I looked inside the bag –
it was a packet of raisins.
How right was that!
I tell children I love raisins so much,
I am Michael Raisin.

The deli at the end of the road
has been renovated:
ceiling painted
the old partition taken down,
floor sanded and polished.
Luckily
no bagels were harmed
in the making of this refurbishment.

Laura Kuenssberg
says the British have a love-hate relationship
with the NHS

I don't have a love-hate relationship
with the NHS
I have a love-love relationship
with the NHS.
If ever I find something wrong
with the NHS
I don't hate it
I care about it
like I might care about someone
who needs more help.

I signed books
for three and a quarter hours
today.
This is my new record.
I was sustained by pieces of melon
and a box of freshly made churros.
There's so much sugar and oil
in them,
I can hibernate till 2029.

The horror. The horror.
I'm think I'm eating something
that is called a bagel
but isn't a bagel.
I have detected that its dough
hasn't been boiled.
This means it's an impostor bagel,
a dissembler, a fraud, a fake,
an impersonator, a cozener
a thing.
A thing
that is nothing more
than a roll with a hole.
The horror.

"Author Michael Rosen wins
Pinter PEN prize for a 'fearless body
of work.'"
At first
I thought that I had been awarded
the 2023 PEN Pinter prize
for a 'fearless body'.

On the Tube tonight
I met Eno
a young writer making waves
in radio, TV, theatre and books.
She was with her cousins and friend
and I got spotted
and we got talking.
Soon coming:
is a book of new writing
edited by
@GeorgeThePoet
 including work by Eno.
Tube as literary salon.

I'm at Virginia School today
and Yumi
has made an overwhelmingly
demanding
cinnamon cake
that shrieks from the table:
Eat me eat me eat me eat me eat me eat me eat me eat me.
I am helping put it out of its misery.

I was doing my shows
at Virginia Primary School today
and one of the teachers told me
that when she was at school,
she was a girl in the same class as Eddie
at Columbia Primary
and she had a photo of the class
when they were in Year 6.
I don't remember
ever having seen the photo before.
There he was on the front row,
sitting on the ground
showing us the soles of his trainers.

I look at his face.
It's that expression
he had when he was listening.
I wasn't there for the photo
but I imagine that I was
and he's listening to me.
That look where he was
intrigued by some nonsense
I was saying
or those times
when he listened to my torment
and told me to walk away from her
and when he gave me the play
he had written
believing that I could put it on
and then when he felt ill
he trusted me to look after him
but in the end
I couldn't
and didn't
in the end.

Occupational therapists
helped me to help myself.
It wasn't their job to 'train' me.
They taught me
how to own my own body,
how to listen to it,
how to learn from it,
how to work it so that it can work.

On my trips to gigs
my tickets are pre-bought.
On Thursday
I followed the routine
at the ticket machine;
my tickets to Newmarket
tumble out,
along with return tickets
to Cambridge.
But I'm not going to Cambridge.
Is the machine telling me
I'm not on my own.
Am I with
someone going to Cambridge
who I don't know about?
I look round.
There's no one there.

The woman in make-up at Channel 5
says
I've got blue skin.

I urged people
to listen to *Word of Mouth* on Radio 4
yesterday.
There was a problem with that.
Word of Mouth wasn't on.
There was no *Word of Mouth* to listen to.
It wasn't listenable.
It was an un-programme.
Not Word of Mouth
was on the radio yesterday.

A man on Euston Station said,
'I was in a coma for 5 days.
How about you?'
'40,' I said.
It felt like I had outscored him.
Man on Euston Station vs Rosen.
Final score: 5-40.
Then I thought
it's probably not helpful
to think in this way.

There's a French guy on this train.
He's talking to someone on his phone.
So now I think I'm on
Le train.

Even if the wrongs
said to have been committed by Jeremy Corbyn
were to be added up,
they are just words.
Unlike the regimes and politicians
he criticises,
he hasn't killed anyone.
Words deemed to be wrong
are, apparently,
much worse than
killing tens of thousands of people.

North London garden:
there used to be song-birds
and pigeons.
Then there were jays
who ate song-bird babies.
Then the jays left.
So it's pigeons now.
And pigeons.

I've found a hair
growing out of the bottom
of my ear lobe.
I don't remember
suggesting to my ear lobe
that it should do this.
I don't remember
making plans
for it to happen.
And yet,
it has.

Everyone has an accent.
It's impossible to speak
without an accent.

Language is not vocabulary.
Vocabulary is not language.
Vocabulary is words.
Language is words-in-syntax-in-context.
Vocabulary is just lists of random words.
We don't speak or write
in lists of random words.
We speak and write in language.

I was in the downstairs loo
with the window open
at the side of the house
and I heard a noise
and for a moment
I thought it was coming from me
(could it be? that loud?)
and I realised
it was next door's strimmer
at work.

I am not at all resentful
that the hole being dug
under a house in our street
is being dug
at seven o'clock
this morning
being dug
being dug
being dug

John has brought his father
to the Eddie memorial hockey match.
To my ear
he sounds Jamaican
when he says to me today,
'I remember the day
I heard that Eddie died.
John told me.
I was driving.
I couldn't believe it.
I just stopped.
Some moments
you never forget.'

In the end
after all the sadness,
for all this time,
24 years since he died,
like John's dad,
all I can say is
I'm bewildered.

I was somewhere.
I bought something.
I filled in a box.
I came home.
Every time I look at my emails,
I get told about something
to do with this place
I once was.
I've forgotten why I was there.
I've never been back.
But I get emails
from them.

There is a fly
on my keyboard.
it has just asked me to explain
the QWERTY arrangement.
I said, it's a long story.
The fly said, 'I'm not in a hurry.'
I said, 'It's to do with Scholes
and then Remington.'
'Ah,' the fly said, 'guns and shavers.'

This is going to be a long night.

Robert Jenrick the immigration minister
orders that a mural of Mickey Mouse
be taken off the wall of an asylum seekers'
reception centre.
The mural was painted over because he thought
they were too welcoming and sent the wrong message.

Paint over Mickey Mouse
Burn *Where the Wild Things Are*
Pulverise the lego
Set fire to the Christmas tree star.

Seize all the teddies
Bury every skipping rope
Paint the walls dark brown
Abolish all hope.

I don't think Robert Jenrick
was painting out Mickey Mouse
because he was taking a critical stance
on the role of Disney in western childhoods.

I wonder
if there are any more murals,
pictures of Micky Mouse
and the like
that will be painted over this week
in refugee centres.
If there are any children's books
in these places,
perhaps they can be burnt.

We are imperfect people
explaining how other people are
imperfect
though some people
have the power
to impose their imperfections
on the rest of us.

Food preparation tip:
When you remove the green leaves
from the top of your strawberries
don't put the leaves in the fruit salad
and throw away the strawberry.

The instruction for my hearing aid battery
asks me to take the sticky label
off the back of the battery
and leave it for a minute
before putting it into the hearing aid.
I watch and wait
staring closely at the battery
breathing
for the first time in its life.

I met someone from Morocco yesterday
and as we walked along Waterloo Road
we ended up speaking in French.
Last night, I dreamt
I was trying to speak French
and someone was saying
that the way I speak French
was full of mistakes, huh!
I remember the 'huh!'
very clearly.

There are times
when the only thing
worth doing next
is to spear an olive.

I said I was dislocated.
I had separated.
I wasn't joined to the person I was.
Trains.
Don't they uncouple or decouple?
I am uncoupled
from who I was.
Detached from me.
My joints
aren't the ones I used to have.
Or it's the way
words come out:
they're sticky.

Sometimes
I find something
in a packet of raisins
that I don't want to describe.

I was sitting under a tree.
A man was asking me to perform
an Elizabethan rap.
He was filming me on a camera
but I had a circular microphone
in my hand.
It looked like a cake.
The language of the rap
was Shakespearian.
I pretended I knew that
Shakespeare wrote raps.
I woke up.

In *Just like Tom Thumb's Blues*
I get it that
it doesn't matter
what each bit means.
It's what it feels like
that matters.
What does
Angel leaving like a ghost
feel like?
Sit in it.
Feel it.
Don't ask it what it is.
To do that is hard.
It means junking 60 years
of analysing.

I wonder how many people
went into a forest
and picked the fruit
in my fruit of the forest ice cream.

Barry tells people Garry is bad.
Barry keeps telling people Garry is bad.
Barry finds different places
to say Garry is bad.
Telling people Garry is bad
proves to Barry that Barry is good.
People say, it's good you told
everyone that Garry is bad, Barry.
Barry feels good.

I'm trying to eat lettuce with a spoon.

I told the story of the coma
and after.
At Q and A time
a man said
it wasn't like that for him.
He was still in the coma.
It felt wrong I had been
chirpy.
I said, see if you can
separate before, during and after.
He sounded like he was
underwater.

The shaman speaks:
You have the power, sir.
You call up ignorant hordes
to do your bidding.
You use your spirit
to conceal the devil
from close inspection.
You deceive
the world into thinking
you have wrought wonders.
I despise people who talk
as I am talking
and yet I do.

The shaman continues:
We are the perfect.
You are the imperfect.
Whenever we identify the imperfect
we nourish our perfectness.
If we find our perfectness
needs reviving
we summon our forces
against the imperfect
drive it out
and our perfectness
is restored.

The shaman reveals:
Only the perfect can see the imperfect.
Beware the false prophet
who hides the work of the anti-god
from the ignorant hordes
Beware the false prophet
who claims
he has seen the imperfect
for the false prophet
will bring down the house of the perfect.

The shaman explains:
the perfect have rules,
the imperfect do not obey the rules.
Though the perfect are perfect
there are times
when the perfect aren't perfect.
But they don't become imperfect.
The perfect are the perfect
because they are the perfect
not because they are perfect.

The shaman points out:
beware the false prophet
summoning the ignorant
to do his bidding.
He deceives the hordes
into thinking his great work
is his genius
when in reality it is
a tawdry patchwork
seized from the labours
of the good and honest
people of the earth.

The people ask the shaman,
how do we know that you are not a false prophet?
The shaman replies:
Because I am one of the perfect. The false prophet is one of the
imperfect and must be cast out.
That is how you know I am one of the perfect.

Some days I work out what else would fit the Beatles phrase
Paperback Writer.
Cucumber raita

Shakespeare knew our smallness:
'our little life is rounded with a sleep.'
It's just a little life.
And then we sleep.
'Out out brief candle.'
He knew.

The grunt hung in the air
looped over the crowd
and landed on the umpire's tray.
The umpire turned it over
gently squeezed it
and shook it in the air.
The crowd waited.
'It's....'
Yes? the crowd wondered.
'...excessive,' the umpire said,
'It's an excessive grunt.'

The pavements were thirsty.
They've had a drink now.
I heard them gulping
and smacking their lips.

I lean out of the shower
to put my hearing aid on the stool.
My feet slide on shampoo dribbles.
I am falling.
I am trying to grab air.
Time passes.
I lose sight of the walls.
There isn't enough power
in my legs.
I collapse
and my tail bone
smacks the shower tray.

It's good to campaign against antisemitism.
One guy did it
by coming to a children's show
I was doing for Jewish Book Week.
Halfway through he stood up
and shouted
'Why do you support Jeremy Corbyn?'
Security escorted him out
and the police were called.
One of the children started crying.
I went on with the show.
Later, he complained
that I used Yiddish in the show.

I had a delicious cake the other day.
The sponge was light and fluffy
and the icing on the cake
was the icing on the cake.

We don't use Ocado.
What happens is that the Offspring
says that he would like some Jaffa Cakes
and Dad (me) goes out and gets them.
It's not Ocado.
It's Odado.

Coming back from the shops
I meet the guy
who lives at the end of the street.
Today
we talk about standing on one leg.
Well, both legs actually
but one leg at a time.
It's a good thing to do,
he says.
I say,
I do it while I'm waiting
for my soup to heat up
in the microwave.

Another guy
campaigned against antisemitism
by telling people that
when he saw me in the street
he booed loudly
and that if his wife
hadn't been with him
he didn't know what he would have done.
He said he knew
where we lived
and offered to call round.

There's an email in my 'junk' folder
from The Horny Milf.
I haven't opened it
but I wondered
if this was a Harry Potter character I missed.

My visit to W. Martyn –
(a shop run by Arsenal-supporting Mr Martyn,
that sells pickles, patés, biscuits, cakes, dried fruit,
and dark chocolate covered ginger) –
ends up today being a long discussion
in which we mix talk of sultanas
with the role of the marauding mid-fielder.

While Ofsted inspectors
are going round schools
telling teachers
that Early Years children mustn't read books
with 'non-decodable' texts,
parents who use libraries
and buy books
are having great fun
reading books with their children at home.

Which is it?
Do I feel foolish or sad
that I didn't start learning Yiddish
while my father was alive?
I imagine us
talking in Yiddish
him correcting me – of course –
laughing and crying
at why his grandfather
would look at good food
and say
'*shnobragants*'
meaning 'goose-beak'.

Today
I went back to St Pancras Rehab Hospital.
There was a bloke in my bed.
I told him.
I said,
'You've nicked my bed.'
He said,
'Sorry, were you in here last week?'
I said, 'No, three years ago.'

The pickled herrings
I buy from my local deli
not only have peppercorns in the brine.
There are cloves.
Sometimes a clove
ends up in my mouth.
At this moment
I have a decision to make:
do I eat the clove
or not?

I'm reeling with shock
and horror.
Man in line at cafe,
looks at bun on display
and says,
'If that's got raisins in it,
I don't want it.'
What?!
The point, surely,
is:
it's only worth having
if it does have raisins
in it.
Things are falling apart
in this country.

Health tip:
for those of you
who have to use eye drops
(as I do),
remember to take your glasses off
before you put the eye drops in your eyes.

When a child
makes an analogy
between an element in a story
and something from their own life
or in another story –
eg the way a character 'helps'
and someone else 'helping',
this is the first step towards
abstract thought.
The power of stories.

I knew a bloke
who was in the building trade
who sang fantastic soul music:
a roofer Franklin.
Steve replied:
There was a guy I knew who was a chippie,
he looked like Elvis.
I replied:
I once ate a chip that looked like Van Morrison.

In spite of the flossing
and vigorous inter-dens work with brushes
that I did last night
(and every night actually),
a tiny piece of ginger
(from the exquisite chocolate ginger I ate)
has just emerged
from between two teeth
on to my tongue.

Writers write puppet-shows.
We never get to see the writers.
Some people think the puppet-show
is the writer.
No.
The puppet-show is what the writer
has written.
The writer is behind the puppet-show
not the show itself.
Then the puppet-show leaves the writer
behind.

He who sees the bottom
of the hummus pot,
knows that he has finished the hummus.

I will be standing in the next election
with a vote-winning slogan
adapted from France.
Mine will be:
Inequality, illegality, inhumanity.

Inequality is what drives ambition and success.
Illegality is what sets us apart from Johnny Foreigner tied up in
red tape.
Inhumanity is how we prove that we protect what we have.
(Er... that is, protect what those who have, have. As it were. Er...)

Am very glad
that there has been a massive focus
on Nigel Farage's human rights.
It means that this will be followed up
with looking at unfair dismissals and evictions,
justice delayed and denied,
and the compensation failures of
Windrush,
Grenfell
and the Post Office,
won't it?

Even the door hinge
squeals a different tune
depending on whether
you're opening
or shutting
the door.

In 1960
at school
we talked of 'trad' jazz, 'modern' jazz
and 'mainstream' jazz.
'Trad' jazz became 'New Orleans' jazz
(which it always was).
I think 'modern' jazz has disappeared
because it's now 'jazz'
and I never knew what 'mainstream' jazz
was anyway.

When the fridges fail in the supermarket
they pull down sheets
and pin up apologies.
First it was the soups bay
Then it was the milks.
Next it was the spreads.
What's next?
Salami?
I'm thinking soon
they'll pull the sheet down outside.
Sorry, the whole place
has failed.

At my show in Frome
I stepped to the front of the stage.
For half a second
I thought I'd leap
into the mosh pit
calling out 'Chocolate Cake – mmmmm'
but then I noticed
everyone was in seats
and the front row
was mums, dads and children
so I decided
it wouldn't be sensible.

I met Paul McCartney for five seconds once.
I was trying to get past him
to record Allen Ginsberg.
He was carrying his guitar.
I said, 'You can play that, can't you?'
He called out to Linda.
'See Linda!
Someone thinks I can play this thing.'

That moment
yesterday
5.30
too late
no bagels left
at the bagel shop.
o woe to the sluggard
who hath not bestirred betimes
to provision himself
with that which he desireth,
as someone famous
should have said.

Peter Hardwick tweeted:
can't you just buy a bun and drill a hole in it?

I replied

A bun is a bun.
A bagel is a bagel.
A bun with a hole in it
is a roll with a hole.
A bagel has been boiled.
First the circle of dough.
Then the boiling.
Then the baking.
Take your bun away, sir
and drill it for as long as you like
but it will never be a bagel.

A super-super injunction
is the injunction
that you can't even say is an injunction.
A super-super-super injunction
is the injunction
to say that you can't say
that there is such a thing
as a super-super-super injunction.
This poem
has just been arrested.

Things that put you off
finishing what you're writing:
I was about 20
and started writing a romantic short story
about a couple called Bruno and Florence.
Someone burst out laughing
at the names.
I didn't finish the story
and have never tried
to write a story like it
since.

I'm filling in a form
to pay a bill.
They ask for 'reference' number.
On the bill it doesn't say 'reference' number.
On the bill it says 'contract' number.
I call.
They say, 'The reference number
is the contract number.'

The man at the crepe and galette stand
at Womad
said, 'Sorry for the delay
in serving you
but we were making the sun-dried tomatoes.'
That would take a long time,
I thought,
especially as it was raining.

One time, when I was seven,
a sixth former, taught by my dad,
babysat my brother and me.
We were bad.
Didn't go to bed.
Went looking for Christmas presents
that we were going to get in a few days' time.
We found them.
She was upset.
Yesterday,
I met her daughter.

I have two puppets:
Old Body and New Body.
Old Body says:
'You love me but you can't have me.'
New Body says:
'You don't love me but you've got me.'
I look round.
Old body's gone.
New Body says,
'I'm here. You can't get rid of me.
We'd better just get on together. '

As a measurement of how woke I am
I was about to have one of my chats
with the bloke at the end of the street
but as I approached
I saw him hide the ciggy he was smoking.
How awful is that?
That's the effect of wokeness.
Merely by appearing
I forced him to deny he was himself.

Every day
I find another hole
in another jumper.
The moths love my jumpers.
I am providing a service to moths.
Moths from all over London
hear about my jumpers.
'Let's go over to Rosen's place
and eat his jumpers.'
'Yeah, c'mon!'
'What do we want?'
'Rosen's jumpers!'

The very first poem I made up
was when I was about seven.
I had an imaginary friend called
Zhonta-bee.
I used to lie in bed chanting,
'How I want to be
a little Zhonta-bee.'

Day 24, US Vice-President
'The Palestinians deserve equal measures of safety and security, self-determination and dignity, and we have been very clear that the rules of war must be adhered to and that there be humanitarian aid that flows.'

I was living in an old house,
someone was telling me
geese and ducks had nests in a tree
and the eggs had hatched.
We went to look.
As we were looking up at the tree
there was a tiger and her cubs
in the tree
and they started to eat the baby birds.

My left eye is crying.
My right eye is not crying.
Half my crying output is working away.
I'm not upset.
I'm not half upset.
I don't mean,
Wow I'm not-half-upset!
I mean
I am not one half upset.
Not 50% upset.
I am
0% upset.

If you wanna boil
Drill for oil.

Some Anaesthetists asked me to give them a one-hour talk
about what it was like being in a coma for 40 days.
I said, 'I don't know.
That stuff you gave me – it worked.'

That was it.
The end.

It was a very short talk.

One morning more.
One more morning
One morning one morning
One more one more
More in the morning
More in the morning
In the morning
there'll be more.
There'll be morning
once more
There'll be more
in the morning.

The chicken soup dilemma.
To make every spoonful
a mix of broth, chicken, carrot and noodle,
Or
to make all the early spoonfuls
mostly broth
and leave
the chicken, carrot and noodle
to the end?
(By the way,
noodles taste better
if you call them *lokshen*.)

After I came out of the coma
the docs told me that I would hallucinate
on account of the 'mind-changing drugs'
they gave me.
i had a few trippy dreams.
That's all.
Last night, three years later,
there was a giant spider-lobster Chewbacca
standing next to my bed.

I thought I could blink it away,
as if it was something on my eye,
but it wouldn't go.
I was afraid to get up and touch it,
in case it was really there.
I did some eye swivelling for a bit
and it shrunk.

There was something in this slice of rye bread.
It wasn't a fingernail.
For a moment it was a fingernail.
Then it was a husk.

I was in a school play
and the teacher directing the play said
that I had to be at the rehearsal
on Tuesday after school.
I said,
'But I do detentions on Tuesdays.'

You know those questions in TV games
when they say,
what four letter words that rhyme
signify a breed of tomato,
a make of helicopter,
a kind of lampshade
and a general in the Austro-Hungarian Empire....
I can NEVER do them.
EVER.

Apostrophes
are
very
hard
to
clean
off
my
computer
screen.

I went to a Jewish picnic today.
I wanted the Yiddish for picnic
to be
pikshnik.
The Yiddish word for picnic is
piknik.

I often call our grater,
the 'grater love hath no man'.
No one thinks that's funny.

Not many people know this
but migrants crossing the channel
brought in ten years of austerity,
wound down the NHS,
put up fuel prices,
caused inflation,
sold off council houses
and partied through the pandemic.

Every household
needs a long-handled teaspoon.
How else is it possible
to get the last of the chutney
out of the chutney jar?

I once met a bloke
who restored old clocks
who said
that he didn't sell a clock
to someone who didn't understand the clock.
It's become a catchphrase in our house:
'But do you understand the clock?'

There is no normal'
says John
I reply:
How dare you?
Our lives rotate around
projecting our view of ourselves
as either being proud that we're normal
or wishing that we were more normal.
It's how we oppress ourselves.
And depress ourselves too,
come to think of it.

Clarification: I did die, but I'm not dead now.

I'm sorry, god knows, I'm sorry
but I was just having some miso soup
when I ate a bit of tofu.
It just went in.
I feel I should apologise to Suella Braverman.
The only thing making it slightly less bad
is that I wasn't reading the *Guardian* at the time.

As a one-off,
why not tweet a volley of abuse at me,
and get blocked?
It passes the time,
keeps me alert.
Makes me feel useful.

In a test on Humpty Dumpty,
if you ask, questions like,
'what did Humpty Dumpty fall off?'
or 'who tried to put Humpty Dumpty back together?'
you can mark it
and fail those who can't answer.

If you ask,
why did Humpty Dumpty fall off the wall?
You get very interesting answers
but
there's no right and wrong answer.

If you make yourself a cup of tea
and leave it in the kitchen
you can't drink it in the living room.

Somewhere
hidden on my keyboard
is a key
that I brush sometimes
unknowingly
and it causes
everything on the screen
to disappear

*

If anyone is interested
in things being a tiny bit more equal,
they'd abolish private education,
tax havens
and increase inheritance tax
for sums above a large amount
(to be agreed on later).
But it's OK,
it won't happen.

In my first week at Oxford Uni, I was fined by the Dean
for making a noise in the quadrangle
after 11pm.
Two weeks later
the rowing guys
made a huge racket past midnight.
They weren't fined.
I asked the Dean why not.
He said,
'You're learning how justice works here, Mr Rosen.'

What if no one was ever 'dumb' again?
People were just 'able'
in different ways?

Ah self-blame:
the most powerful tool
that our rulers have at their disposal.

I once made the mistake
of answering a question
in an English exam
totally honestly.
I thought the 'unseen' poem
was sentimental and clichéd
and I said so.
Turned out,
it was a 'classic'
and classic poems are 'great',
so I was wrong.

Spreading hummus on a bagel
I think that it is a matter
of will there be enough hummus
for the bagel
or enough bagel
for the hummus?

There is always a lost record.
A lost vinyl.
Whatever they are
there's always a lost one.
I flick through them on the shelf
looking for the one I scratched to hell
in that flat by the canal.
Did I lend it to someone?
Doesn't matter if I did.
It's the one that's not there.

Judge: You are hereby found guilty of the crime of Being Bad.
Defendant: There's no such crime.
Judge: I decide what is a crime.
Defendant: How's that fair?
Judge: I only name what can be reasonably called a crime.
Defendant: '...can be reasonably called'? Who by?
Judge: Me.

If I saw you –
a thing I say to myself
on buses and trains
I would say:
I never said thank you
I would say
I never said sorry.

I often forget to say thank you.
I guess that's not kind.
I often forget to say sorry
I guess that's not good.
What I did and didn't do
was not good too
but not saying sorry
makes it worse.

I went to the moon
in our coal bunker
I controlled the space ship
and navigated it too.
There were problems with the engine.
I solved those.
A dangerous asteroid headed towards us.
I veered away.
I looked up.
My father had been watching me
since I took off from the launch pad.

A lot of my father's life
seemed to revolve round his *kishkes*.
As in 'It's bad for my *kishkes*',
'he bust his *kishkes* to do that',
'it's gone straight through my *kishkes*',
'I can't drink that, it plays hell with my *kishkes*'.

My brother told me that
the stuff on our bedroom walls
was 'distemper'.
When my friend Harrybo came over
I showed him
how if you licked your finger
you could make stripes
in the distemper.
Later, my father said,
'What are these stripes?'
I said, 'I dunno.'

At the back of the cupboard
I found a jar with a little bit of granola in it.
I thought,
Don't be shy, little granola,
out you come,
I've got just the place for you,
c'mon granoly, oly noly.

I don't think it was expecting this –
it had been pretty quiet for years
I ate it.

The Kindness of Strangers?
No.
It's the Illness of Strangers now.
Strangers spot me and in seconds
we are swapping
defective thyroid glands
knees with pseudo gout
divergent eyeballs
gigantic prostate glands
and doing The Plank.
Then we congratulate each other
we're living.

My mother would say
'I was emergency trained.'
She said, that after the war
they were short of teachers
so she left her job at Kodak
and trained miles away
in a stately home.
I went there for her end of course show.
It was on the wall.
I was 3.
I can still see
how proud she was.

As the Bomb fell on Hiroshima
my father was in the US Army
teaching troops in Shrivenham, Oxfordshire.
He had come to England when he was two
so in his head he was
a kid from London's East End,
a scholarship boy
and a Communist.
Sometimes he said to himself
'Why am I here?'

When I went out walking
with my father
down the long suburban roads
where the lights never came on
in the front rooms,
my father would say to me,
'Why do we live in this place, Mick?'
And I'd say,
I don't know.
I'm seven
It's not my fault we live here.
Why are you asking me?

My father could become
an American in the American Army:
being shouted at by the top sergeant
to get up in the morning:
'Shit, shine, shave and shower!'
Say it again, I'd say,
'Shit, shine, shave and shower!'
Then I said it in school.
'Where did you get that?'
they'd say.

My mother would say to me
as I was going to school
'You don't want to go out
looking like a *shloch*.'
I'd say
'What's a *shloch*?'
and she'd say,
'The thing you don't want to look like.

At times my father would swear in Yiddish:
'*ch'adich im loch*!'
My mother furious at him,
'Don't say that Harold!'
We say:
'What did he say?
What did he say?'
My mother says:
'Don't tell them, Harold.'
And he never did.

Long after my mother was gone
I asked my father, what did that
''ch 'a' dich im loch' thing mean
that you used to say
that mum said you shouldn't say?
He said, 'It means:
'I've got you in my hole.''
What?!
What hole?
And why had my father got someone in it?

It was very difficult
teaching suburban kids in 1956:
we didn't all come in on the right beat
at the beginning of
'For all the saints...'
Our teacher used to slam her hymn book down
(for the beat)
Boom!
'For all the saints...'
We never got it.
She was livid.

When I was six
a boy came up to me in the playground
and said,
'You're Jewish, aren't you?'
I said yes
so he said that his mum said
that I ought to go to Hebrew Classes.
I said to my Communist atheist Mum
'I'm going to Hebrew Classes.'
'That's nice,' she said.
So I went.

Our German teacher kept giggling.
She taught us Brahms' lullaby:
'Guten Abend, gut' Nacht
mit Rosen bedacht...'
Then she giggled.
'Rosen', she said.
'Yes', I thought,
'you taught with my father, you taught my brother,
now you're teaching me.
It's lasted a long time, this joke.'

When an empty chair creaks.
Not just once.
Twice.
Three times.
No one's there.
A chair
deciding it wants to creak.
So it creaks.

I was standing in the Arsenal shop
A man I'd never seen before
said to me, 'It was my great grandfather's fault
your father didn't get a bar mitzvah suit.'
I said, 'The suit that his uncle promised him?'
He said, 'Yes.'
'It's OK,' I said,
'his grandfather made it for him.'

I never knew
what 'You're in disgrace' meant.
They used to say that to us
at school.
'You're in disgrace!'
Where was this place – 'disgrace'?
Wherever it was
you could easily be 'in' it.
And it was bad.
It was a bad place to be in.
But where was it?

I didn't need to cut my toenails
before we went to an art gallery today
but I thought it would
improve the experience.

At the Royal Academy Summer Exhibition
there was a robot who did a V-sign at me
a girl who was too big to fit in the frame
a window with a shirt you could see through
I imagined an egg-box full of glass eyeballs
and a woman came up to me
and said that she had a plastic aorta.

Hot water for the bath
came from what my parents called
'the geyser',
a white cylinder
fixed above the bath
a silver pipe pointing downwards
caked with lime scale at the end
it boomed and coughed
and wore a badge saying
'Ascot'.
In a window on the front
if you looked in
there was a blue light
that never went out.

On our Hoover at home
(1950s)
it said in white letters
'It beats
as it sweeps
as it cleans.'

My father talked of foods
that came from a place
called 'Before the War'.
'Ah, my Bubbe's *cholent*!' he says,
And Mum says,
'Well, I'm not your Bubbe.
She spoiled you.
Don't you go thinking
 I'm going to stand by the cooker
for 24 hours cooking you *cholent*
like your Bubbe did.'

'Don't tell your mother
I told you this
but one time she had to take flowers
for Harvest Festival at school.
All they had was a back yard.
So she nipped to the park
by the Museum
and took in a flower from there.
Your mother, a '*ganuf*'!
Don't you go telling her
I told you this.'

If I didn't do my homework
my mum would say,
'Do your homework.
You don't want to end up like the Michaelsons.'
'The Michaelsons?' I'd say
'Who are the Michaelsons?
I've never met the Michaelsons.'
'The Michaelsons were so poor,' my Mum said, 'Mr Michaelson
didn't even own a stall in the market
he was just a *shlepper*.'
'A shlepper? What's a *shlepper*?' I said.
'The man who takes the stuff
from the lorry to the stall.
That's all he was – a *shlepper*.
Do you want to end up being a *shlepper*?'
What was she talking about?
We lived in Pinner.
Long rows of suburban houses
where the lights never came on
in the front rooms.
Market stalls?
There were no market stalls in Pinner
let alone men taking stuff TO the stalls.
Of course I wasn't going to end up
being a *shlepper*.

All year we did 'Clause Analysis'
Mrs Turnbull had a fail-safe method:
learn the conjunctions that start the clause:
if, although, when... every lesson.
We went into the exam:
Clause Analysis:
But the clause began, 'no matter...'
We looked across the Hall at each other.
Wossthis?

My father liked to fry liver and onions.
The thing is
we had an airer.
A horizontal clothes-horse
that they hoisted up to the ceiling
with a rope and pulley,
tied off on a hook by the kitchen door.
The clothes dried very well on the airer
and often smelled of
liver and onions.

'Mum, the milk's gone sour.
It smells of sick.
I'll chuck it down the sink'
'No, don't do that...' she said.
She poured it into a bowl
and stood in the kitchen
spooning it into her mouth,
rolling the lumpy bits on her tongue,
'Mmmm,' she said.
'Mum's eating sick.' I said.

Every few months
Mr Weston came over with his moustache
and a leather case full of brushes
for our Hoover.
My brother and his son were friends.
They used to sing a song about Sharp's Toffee.
'Stro-o-o-ng toffee!'
Whenever I ate Sharp's Toffee
I thought of Hoover brushes.

We weren't a religious family
though my father worshipped
the stove in the front room.
Made by Courtier, Mick, he said.
He often explained its secret ways to me.
He twisted the air flow control.
He riddled the grate.
He taught me how to peer through the windows
to see the holy glow inside.

I keep thinking of a painting
in the exhibition yesterday:
a back room
opening out on to a garden;
hanging from the ceiling
a shirt
so thin and pale
you could see through it
into the garden.
I've decided that it belonged to a man
who's just died.

My brother was in the School Choir.
They sang 'The Messiah'.
He practised at home.
There was one bit that made Mum laugh.
She walked round the house
doing a sad clown face, singing it:
'All we like sheep have gone astray-ay-ay-ay'
Why did she think that was funny?

I think my mother found it comical
when she came across lines in religions
that suggested we are less than we are
or that we should be satisfied with our lot.
One of her favourites was:
'Let self-sacrifice be its own reward.'
That one made her giggle.

My Sixth Form form teacher
who had a strong Welsh accent
and was very short-sighted
would call out my name from the register
and when there was no answer,
he would look vaguely into the distance
and then say, 'Ah, one of Rosen's long weekends, is it?'

Once a week
on the radio:
'Journey into SPA-A-ACE!'
After it was over
my brother went upstairs
to our bedroom
and acted it out, under the covers,
using cupped hands for the echo effect.
'Go back-ack-ack-ack!
Go back-ack-ack-ack!'
'Lemmy?
Are you there, Lemmy?
Lemmy?
Lemmy?'

It was my job to put shillings and half-crowns
in the gas meter.
A man often came over
piled the coins up on the kitchen table
in silver columns,
wrote figures in a leather book.
then swept the coins into a bag,
though some he gave back to us.
Felt like he was giving us money.

My mother explained
that we owned the Co-op.
That's why I had to take the shopping list
and the 'trundle'
all the way down Marsh Road
to a small dark shop at the end.
I often went with her to
the National Provincial Bank.
I said, 'Do we own this one as well?'
'No,' she said.

There was a builder's yard
out the back of our place.
On Sundays
my father and I visited the dump.
He'd spot a window-frame.
'Grab that, Mick,' he'd say.
When we went in,
he'd say, 'We got a great window-frame today, Connie.'
She'd say, 'What's that for?'
He'd say, 'Not sure yet.'

In the International Stores
there were glass topped boxes
for biscuits
bills flew across the ceiling
in metal cars on wires
to Mrs Calvert in the kiosk.
Her son Johnny played out with us.
He fell off the roof
of the International Stores
and he didn't play out anymore.

At Bubbe's house
there was a ship in a bottle on the mantlepiece
a ship with funnels on a painted sea.
They'd all been on ships with funnels
from the '*heim*' to here.
Or my father
with his mother, sister and baby brother
from America
not knowing he'd never see his father again.

I told Mum that me and the others at school
were fed up with the bus strike.
She handed me a tenner
'Put it in the bucket
at the bus garage.'
How do you know there's a bucket? I said.
'It's for the strike fund.'
She was right.
I put the tenner in the bucket
in my school uniform.

My father never let a moment go by
without using it to raise my consciousness.
I was chosen to read for the Service of Nine Lessons.
He heard me:
'There went out a decree from Caesar Augustus that all the
world should be taxed.'
'Quite,' he said, 'what does that tell you, eh?'

Every New Year we went to a party
where grown-ups told jokes
There was Malcolm with a voice.
He was in Radio Drama.
There was Francis who was Armenian.
He did the Archibald Arseolein one.
There was Solly.
He'd once shouted at the Home Secretary.
He told very long Jewish jokes.

My father fried corned beef
with baked beans.*
'What's that?' I said
'Chazze bupkes,' he said.
'What's 'chazze bupkes?' I said.
'Tiger's eggs,' he said.
'What's tiger's eggs?'
'Chazze bupkes,' he said.
Then he served it up.
It was delicious.
'So you like *chazze bupkes*?' he said.

'If the engine on a Doodlebug cut out
it meant it was going to land
so you had to get somewhere safe
so if you were in the street
they said, 'Lie down in the gutter.'
I came out of White City Station,
there was a Doodlebug coming over
so I lay down in the gutter,'
Mum said.

The first time I went to America
I was at a conference in Orlando.
There was a buffet lunch.
I thought that I could fit in
with that easily enough.
I sat down with my plate of food.
The person next to me was
eating alligator with strawberries.

Our new French teacher
said that we would learn a lovely little French song
about a little sailor boy.
We sang it.
The boy is about to be eaten by the other sailors
who discuss how to cook him
and what sauce to use.
It's got a lovely jolly little chorus.

One of the boys in my class at school
became an artist
with shows in a London gallery.
He got to be good at art
because he practised
while he was at school
by drawing pictures of a toilet
with the chemistry teacher's head
peeping out of the toilet bowl.

Secondary Modern Schools had a grammar school stream.
Grammar Schools had facilities for 'domestic science' and
'woodwork'.
In Woodwork
I spent a whole year not making a stool.
At the end of the year, I went home with what I had started
with:
4 long bits of wood and 1 flat bit.

A bowl that had cornflakes in it
came out of the dishwashing experience
with two cornflakes still stuck to it.
As an experiment
I put the bowl in for a second
dishwashing experience.
It came out with the same two cornflakes
still stuck to it.

One time I came back from university
and was moaning to Mum
that a script for a little sketch I had written
but not directed
had ended up being a flop
and she said,
'You've got to remember that in some people's hands
even the best things can be turned to *dreck*.'

If the arts had the same tradition as the sciences
when it comes to naming,
then things like a 'metaphor' would be named after people:
'that's a great Aristotle in the third line,'
A pause in dialogue in drama would be a Pinter.
'One particular poignant Pinter was when Lady Macbeth
couldn't find her hairbrush.'

They knew how to make a subject thrilling
at Grammar schools in the old days.
The first lesson in Chemistry was
the Bunsen Burner.
We looked at the Bunsen Burner.
We were told the name of each part of the Bunsen Burner
They said, Now draw the Bunsen Burner
labelling it
correctly.

Yesterday
I treated myself to a packet of Liquorice Allsorts.
But I encountered a problem:
what do you call one of them?
It can't be an 'allsort' because
one of them is only one sort.
So is one of them a 'sort'?
I've stopped eating them
while I try to figure that one out.

asbestos pad
on our ironing board
wearing away;
fibres floating through evening meals
riding kitchen thermals
in the fog
of my parents' cigarette smoke.
It was pleasing to find that
pushing my finger on the pad
made minute asbestos sausages
that I could flick
onto the floor.

My father sometimes said things
that were utterly mysterious.
'You see, Mick, your mother
puts egg in the pastry.
You won't get that round your friends' houses.'
What?
Why wouldn't I get egg in pastry
round at my friends' houses?
But I just nodded.
Right. OK. Yes.

Which of the two do I feel fondest about?
Meg who thinks I'm Mum
sits on my lap purring
nodding at my hand when she wants more
ear tickles?
Jack who sits near rather than on,
or who, when he sits
walks about on me
dodging strokes
showing me he is who he is
how he wants to be?

Once in France
when I was seventeen
I was staying in the house of a French professor
of Italian.
In one of Pavese's poems was the line 'Ripeness is all' in English (from
King Lear).
He asked me what it meant.
I said 'maturity'.
I've just found out I was wrong.
It meant 'readiness'.

Word of the day is 'inadvertently'.
Mr Sunak inadvertently failed to declare an interest.
This needs to be taught to school students for their excuses:
'Sorry, Miss, I inadvertently punched him.'
'Sorry, I was inadvertently at home yesterday.'

A woman just stopped me in the street
and said,
'You're my greatest fan.'
I said, 'I don't think so.
I've never met you before.'

I told her that
a boy once saw me on the bus
and said,
'You're fingy, innit?'
I said, 'Yes.'
and he said, 'I thought so.'

I told her that once
a boy said to me,
'Are you, Michael Rosen?'
I said, 'Yes.
And he said, 'Yes,
you look just like him.'

On Seaford Beach
I started to count the pebbles.
I got to 15
and fell asleep.

On the M25
yesterday
a moment
between signs
I wonder, where are we?
No way of knowing.
We are
in M25 land
a country of cars
outside
and just the two of us
inside.
Neither here
nor there.
Rushing between.

Lying on my back
breathing out for as far
as possible
and further.
And further.
Stop.
Keeping the position of my back
and chest
when breathing in.
Bit
by
bit
my
back
flattennnnnnns.

Poetry – don't go near it.
Best thing to do, is fear it.
It's not funny.
It doesn't make money
And when poets read,
you can't hear it.

There are always traces.
The keys on my computer rattle
more than they used to.
I'm puzzled.
I summon up possible causes.
A glass of orange juice
emerges.
I see my hand hit it.
(part of my still-not-understood
wonky vision,
covid bleeds on the optic nerve)
Juice on the keys.

Michael,
remember to keep your right eye
(the good one)
open wide
otherwise
the good right eye
ends up imitating
the blurry eye
the one with hardly any vision
the left one.
'Look at me,' says the good eye,
'I can do blurry too,' it says.

I bought a new pair of shoes.
My daughter said, 'They're huge,
they're bigger than your last ones.'
My wife came in.
She said, 'Those shoes look smaller
than your others.'
I know the truth
but I'm not saying.

A mother and her two boys
stopped me at Kings Cross Station
this evening.
The woman said
they were from Newcastle and
that she recognised me
but said she didn't know my name
and the boy shouted,
'I know you. You're the rhymer.'

A suggestion from an editor of a draft of a children's book
you're working on:
'Do you think you could make it a bit sillier?'
'I'll see what I can do.' I say.

My friend Brian Harrison
told me when we were boys
that his grandmother
(born in the 1870s in Gillingham Kent)
called a fart, a 'windypop'.
My mother
(born 1919 in London (East End)
called a fart, a '*fotz*'
(Yiddish).
Brian Harrison and I
had interesting conversations.

We found a caterpillar on the stairs.
I put it out the window.
An hour later
it was back.
I had a word with it:
a brief speech about
wrong place wrong time.

I have a new trick.
I am working in a building.
People say goodbye to me.
I look for the stairs.
I go down to the bottom
I find myself face to face with a fire exit door.
I open it.
An alarm goes off.
I close it.
A few days later:
I am working in a building –
repeat, as before.

I was standing by Reception
at the Whittington Hospital today
and a Chinese guy called Roland
came past pushing an empty wheelchair.
He held up his phone
and asked me to say
'Nice!'.
I said,
'Nice!'

I wonder how an old schoolfriend is doing.
Last time I had an email chat
was 15 years ago.
I write.
My email account
tells me that my email
can't be delivered.

All day in A and E (not for me).
Around us
the non-stop solid slog
of listening to people's pain
coming up with ways to soothe and mend
name after name after name
a woman's broken toe
a man who says he'll sue
and a woman who says
it's 1923.
The long time of now.

The offspring
lays on a feast for himself.
I look at it with yearning.
No go.
But no need to be down about it.
I know that in the morning
there will be leftovers
for me to
gorge on.

The guy in the car
was saying
that there are red buses and yellow buses
and blue buses
and these buses are all fine with that
and what's more
they leave each other alone.
A red bus went past.
I looked at it closely.
It seemed fine about being red.
He was right.

When I get emails from my French friends
I get a message across the top that says,
'Translate message to English; Never translate from French'
That second bit seems very harsh.
It sounds like someone in my server
is either grumpy or xenophobic.

The reason why my glasses case is empty
is because
I'm wearing my glasses.

I ate my thyroid gland.
Well, my antibodies did:
Y-shaped proteins
that identify and neutralise foreign objects.
At some point my antibodies
had the inclination to regard my thyroid
as one of these foreign objects.
I'm not sure
I agree with the politics of this.

I worked in a school in the late 1970s
and there was a boy
who sat at the back of the class
doing Bruce Lee moves.
Over two terms,
I don't know many invisible foes he dealt with.
Hundreds probably.
'Remember,' he said to me,
'be shapeless, like water.'
'I'll try,' I said.

On a raft.
Out at sea.
Hot sun.
Towels.
I say, 'Let's get under the towels.'
No food.
I plan to distil sea water on a plate.
Night comes.
'What do we sleep on?' I say.
'The towels,' they say.
'Then there's nothing over us,' I say.
'What do you expect?' they say.

I've just heard the phrase
'...whose head resides inside the toilet...'
from the telly
(being watched by someone else
on the other side of the room)
I'm worried now.

I know the danger:
eating late at night
and demon indigestion.
I once ate mushrooms at 1am.
Agony.
Last night:
big risk – an onion bhaji
dipped in hummus.
I shouldn't have done it.
I knew the risk.
But I did it anyway.
Yet
and yet
I survived,
without a murmur from
in there.

We went to see my father's cousin Ted
in America.
He was 101.
I asked him how he was feeling.
'Resigned,' he said.

I'm not sure
if that noise is
a gale through the trees
a wind howling down the gutters
a storm spiralling in the chimney
or the dishwasher.

I've picked up an earlier train than the one I was due to catch.
It's a train that's delayed by three hours.
Everyone on the train is looking very fed up
except for me who thinks he's early.
Did Einstein have something to say about this?
Perhaps not.

The woman doing tickets
on the train has just said,
'I'm in stealth mode.
I'm a creeping shadow'.

A girl came up to me in Leeds Museum
and said she liked my poem 'No Breathing'.
I said, thanks,
She started doing it,
imitating my voice and gestures.
It was like I was looking at me
as an eight-year-old girl.
Uncanny.

Yesterday,
I was in a children's dialysis ward
at Leeds Children's Hospital.
What a reminder of life
and how the NHS was created to fight for it.

One of my fingers
finds a key
that sends an email
that I'm replying to
straight off to 'Archive'.
There's an intention to this.
Something thinks that
halfway through a sentence
I should be archived,
made history,
filed away.
I go to Archive.
I retrieve.
I resist.

I heard a scuffle at the patio door.
I know what it is.
The cats chase flies up the glass.
I look.
Ah no, it's next-door neighbour's cat outside.
Ah no, it's a fox.
The cats look at it as if to say
'Yeah we have trouble with him most days.
Ignore him. He'll go away.'
He did.

On my way through Ally Pally Park this morning,
I met a rat.
It said, 'I'm looking for organic matter of any kind.
I'm not picky. Go away and leave me alone.'

The pitted prune
buried in the deep of the oats,
its succulence contrasting
with the flakiness,
the bite
the release
but then -
the unpitted pitted prune
strikes.
The stark rigid clash.
The jolt.
The intrusion
into pleasure.
How dare it do that?

Sometimes I peer into
my mostly faded eye
and feel I'm falling into it
drawn down a well
head first
arms sucked in
legs flailing
then gone.

If you build a house invisibly
no one will care very much
about pulling it down.

Me to Me: What do you do when you finish one pot of
hummus?
Me in reply to Me: Open another one immediately?
Me to Me: Correct.

The problem with News,
is that it's News.
It's endlessly new.
It endlessly displays
its now-ness.
It endlessly displays events,
it defines reality
as events,
reality as moments,
though there is
just time between the moments
for hosts
to demand yes/no?
bad/good?
like/hate?
Sorry that's all we have time for.
And then it's over to Jack
for the weather.
Hello Jack.

If I'm mistyping,
I sometimes turn 'hello' into 'gecko'.
Gecko
would make a good greeting.

For people who like treasure hunts,
can I recommend trying to find the toilets
on Finsbury Park Station?
In a tunnel below the platforms,
there's a sign for them
but the signs run out
and you don't know whether
to go forwards, backwards
up to the platforms,
wet yourself,
or die.

I've got a new set of earphones.
I wonder how soon I'll lose this pair too.

In the night
my leg said
'Wake up. Wake up.'
I said, 'What?
Why are you waking me up?
I'm not going anywhere today.
I don't have to get up early.
I don't want to get up now.'
'No,' my leg said,
'I'm cold.'

If you make lecture notes
on a piece of paper
with a shopping list on it
you an easily mix up
things like
hermeneutics
with break, milk and tomatoes.

A poem can be
what you see.
A poem can tell
of what you
touch, taste or smell.
A poem can imagine
or remember
or investigate.
You can write it
early
You can write it
late.

He realised he had to wait
and there was always
someone ahead of him in the line
and it didn't matter.
Saying to himself, 'it didn't matter'
was not a giving-in thing.
It was that he could feel stronger
knowing that
he didn't have to get racked up about it.

I missed April and May 2020.
It seems a bit careless.

There's a group of harm-wishers
who get their fix
dishing out psychobabble
and malevolent adjective diarrhoea.

I wonder if there's medication
you can take for
malevolent adjective diarrhoea.

What is your Day One?
When is your Day One?
It seems that the press decide for us.
Their timeline starts
where they choose it to start.
Once they've chosen,
they ask people,
'Do you condemn Day One?'
Some people say, Yes!
I condemn Day One!
Others want to say
that their Day One is different
and they want to condemn
all the Day Ones.
They are quickly derided
for being deniers
and condoners.

Lines from a ten-year-old
in a poetry workshop today:
'Feel your heart
inside the word.'

Sometimes,
when the people backstage say to me,
you've got 1500 children out there,
they're under-8
and you've got them for an hour,
I think...but have I got
an hours' worth of things in my head
for 1500 under-8s to be entertained?
Have I?

Someone came up to me today
and said,
'You're the guy off tik-tok, aren't you?'
I don't even know what tik-tok is,
let alone whether
I'm on it
or not.

you roll over quickly in the bed
and you're hit with the room spinning
and a sick thing grabs your throat
and your stomach shrinks
and rocks
and you sit up
and the room is still spinning
and spinning
and spinning

Someone has written to me
and signed off with
'All the vest'.
It's a typo apparently.
The person has written me
another letter to apologise.
I've said, 'Don't worry.
I love 'all the vest'.'
And why not 'all the vest', anyway?
The weather's on the turn.

I'll be talking to 800 health professionals
later today.
If I had 800 symptoms of something
I could get each one looked at.

I was typing out some Shakespeare today.
Cleopatra: 'O Charmian,
where think'st thou he is now? Stands he, or sits he?'
but text predict says that Charmian should be Chairman.
Changes the meaning a bit:
'O Chairman, where think'st though he is now?'

Whose body is this?
It's a dead body.
Here is another dead body.
They have both been killed.
Shall we say
that we regret that both
people have been killed
or shall we say
that we regret the death
of one
more than the other?

The sound of rain stopping.
The sound of lessening.
The sound of abating.
The sound of nothing.
The sound of the memory of rain.

People are being killed
and politicians tell us
that people could be killed.
A humanitarian disaster is taking place
and politicians tell us
that a humanitarian disaster
could take place.
The politicians have changed time:
they've moved the present to the future.

You will not compare numbers.
A larger number
is no longer a larger number.
A larger number
is not a number.
A larger number
does not exist.
There is no such thing
as a larger number.
You will not talk
of larger numbers.
To talk of larger numbers
threatens us.
Talking of larger numbers
denies our right to exist.
Talking of larger numbers
is banned.

That hour between the time
you take your thyroxine
and you have breakfast.
It's
a
long
hour.

When they said
that Israel had a right to defend itself
they weren't saying
that Israel could kill 5000 people.
They were saying
that Israel had the right to defend itself.
This means
that it's OK to kill 5000 people.

We want bread, said the peasant,
we're starving.
I am merciful, said the King,
we will announce today
that the people might starve soon.
But we're starving now, said the peasant.
I am merciful, said the King,
I promise we will announce
that the people might starve.

The King's tutor said,
'Here are 5 apples
here are 20 apples,
which basket holds the most apples?'
The king took the 20 apples
out of the basket
and replaced them with 20 oranges.
'The basket with 5 apples in it
holds the most apples,'
he said.

'When did the world begin?'
said the King's tutor.
'The world began yesterday,' said the King.
'That's not strictly true,' said the tutor.
'It may not be strictly true,' said the King,
'But you will say that it's true.'
The tutor said nothing.
'Go on, say it,' said the King.
'The world began yesterday,' said the tutor.
'Correct,' said the King.

'I don't know what to say to the people,'
said the King.
'Fluffy white clouds,' said the tutor.
'Just that?' said the King.
'Say, 'what do we want?
Fluffy white clouds.
When do we want them?
Now.'
'Why should I say that?'
'It shows you believe
in fluffy white clouds,'
the tutor said.
'But I don't believe in
fluffy white clouds,'
said the King.
'Why's that relevant?'
said the tutor.

The great thing about twitter
is that one day
I might hit someone with news about
semi occluded vocal tract exercises
for muscle tension dysphonia
and a few days later
someone hits me with
benign paroxysmal positional vertigo.

I dreamed that
someone told me that in French,
to 'steer' a car is *'cuire'*.
I said, 'But *'cuire'* means to 'cook'.'
And they said,
'Isn't it interesting that
 it's the same word?
In a way when you steer a car
you're cooking a car?'
I thought, is it?

A child asked me what subject was I good at, at school.
I said, 'Daydreaming'.
Daydreaming helps you write.
It should be put on the National Curriculum.
You daydream.
You then write what you were daydreaming.
Or: you're given a subject.
You daydream about it.
You write it.

There are MPs who object
to the fact
that there are streets
where people speak a language
other than English.
My mother and father
grew up in streets like that.
They both became teachers,
my mother in a primary school.
My father taught English.

The King's tutor said
'You must keep telling the people that it's going to be good very soon.'
'I know,' said the King, 'I've been doing that for years. Won't they notice that all the time I've been saying it's going to be good, it hasn't been good?'
'Some people notice,' said the tutor, 'but we'll call them names and people will hate them. That way, everyone will be rowing about whether people are good or bad and not about whether things are good or not.'
'Is there a name for this?' said the King.
'Yes,' said the tutor, 'it comes from grammar. We call it the 'future present'. We arrange it so that everyone lives in the future present.'

They have found a new way
to not notice.
They say,
Rage at the words
Rage at what people say
Rage at what people write
and
deaths will slip away
like shadows when the sun rises.
No one will notice
but they'll rage at the words
rage at what people say
rage at what people write.

Lo! and I will plead with the plebs
to not sink to the level of treating this terrible crisis
as if it's a football match.
Lo! I will show them it's not a crude matter
of taking sides.
Lo! I will write harsh words about people
who have not condemned what should be condemned
Lo! I will explain how one side has suffered
Lo! No one will notice that I have taken sides
and written as if it's a football match
Lo! I speak.

When we say 'the clocks go back tonight'
I've noticed
that some of our clocks go back
and some don't.
Clocks discuss this:
'I'm going back.'
'I'm not.'
'Do you think you're some kind of rebel?'
'What's the matter with you?'
'No. What's the matter with YOU?'

'What you say, sir, is that you're being reasonable,' said the
King's tutor.
'I get that,' said the King, 'but what if I know that I'm being
unreasonable?'
'You just keep saying you're being reasonable,' said the tutor.
'But what if people say that I'm being unreasonable?' said the
King.
'You say, 'Surely it's not possible for me to be unreasonable if
I've said that I'm being reasonable', said the tutor.

The worse it gets in Gaza,
the louder they shout about the antisemitism
they're suffering.

I like mysteries.
Here's some:
why is the American Secretary of State
spending many hours of his time
rushing round the Middle East?
Why do we think this fact is so unremarkable
that we don't ask why he is doing this?
Is it an act of nature,
like the seasonal winds that
blow round the earth?
What has this place,
thousands of miles from the American borders
got to do with America?
What is his purpose?

The press are very interested in longterm objectives.
They inform us that the longterm objectives
of Hamas is the annihilation of the state of Israel.
Do they also tell us of the longterm objectives
of the Israeli government?
What are the views of the Israeli government
towards the West Bank, Gaza, the Golan Heights
and Lebanon?
What does the phrase 'ancestral lands'
mean?
What policies, what military activity
will be needed to carry out these
longterm objectives?

To make up for turning the clock back
I got up early
so now it's yesterday.

I was fourteen.
I got out of the pool
and my swimming teacher said
'You're putting all your effort into breathing in.
Make sure you breathe everything out
and the breathing in will look after itself.'

Wars love civilians.
Wars feed off civilians.
Wars devour civilians.
Wars crush civilians.
Wars blame civilians
for being there.
Wars remove civilians.
Then wars improved.
Wars became wars
over which civilians
are the most entitled to die.
Wars improved.
Wars are much better these days.

While the death toll
goes from
one thousand
to two thousand
to three thousand
to ten thousand
the US Secretary of State
is telling us over and over again
that he is urging the Israelis
to minimise the deaths.
People will be glad
that so much was done
to keep numbers so low.

I asked the rain to stop before I go out.
It has.
Cause and effect.
Science.

'The Emperor says we must minimise deaths', said the King's tutor.

'Very good,' said the King, 'anything else?'

'He says we have the right to do be doing what we're doing,' said the tutor.

'Very good,' said the King, 'but are we minimising deaths?'

'I don't think so,' said the tutor.

'So we're not doing what the Emperor wants us to do,' said the King.

'I think, your majesty, it's more about what the Emperor wants to look like he's doing,' said the tutor.

'Oh, is he minimising deaths, then?' said the King.

'No,' said the tutor, 'he wants to look like he's doing what he can to minimise deaths.'

'But I thought he said that I have the right to be doing what I'm doing,' said the King, 'which is not minimising deaths.'

'It's very complicated,' said the King's tutor, 'but yes.'

I keep muddling GM with AI.
It means I worry about
big talking tomatoes.

the get-up
the morning chill
the return into
the shape of yourself
in the bed
the heat of yourself
in the bed
waiting for you
to come home.

you know when you're older
than you were
is when it doesn't matter anymore
that Sunday night
comes before Monday morning.

If there's an elephant in the room
how can there be room for
the grown-ups in the room?

The world leaders watch the war
and weep for the dead.
They are sorry for the killing
though some point out
it's a fact
that when you're fighting evil
sometimes babies have to die.
The world leaders agree
that the best way to help
would be for there to be a
humanitarian minute
between agreed times when
it's reasonable for babies
to be killed.

News that made daily headlines in 2020
is being unravelled and exposed at the Covid Inquiry
but many of these once-huge moments
are hardly being covered by the papers and TV now.
In the 24-hour News cycle,
it's not news.
Matters of life or death for 1000s?
Not interested.

At school
our teacher told us
that squirrels hoard acorns
so that when they wake up
from hibernation
there'll be a feast waiting for them.
Rather like me buying raisins yesterday
and waking up this morning.

Every morning
the dilemma:
I go to the cupboard
pluck a dried fig from the packet,
pull off the stalk
and debate whether to walk over to the bin
with the stalk
or put it back in the packet,
as I have other delights to grab
from in the cupboard too...

My father was a teacher,
a teacher-trainer,
a linguist,
a polyglot,
an educational theorist,
an expert on narrative
and on folk literature
and he could put his finger in his ear and waggle it so
vigorously that his ear squeaked loud enough to be heard across
a room.

I was in the Kings Arms in Oxford yesterday
and was shocked to see that the menu for bar food
had changed since last time I looked
which was in 1969.

Worried that quite a few animals
are being named after Attenborough.
Am imagining them meeting up:
'Hi, who are you?'
'I'm Attenborough.'
'You're Attenborough? No, I'm Attenborough.'
'Hold it you two, I'm Attenborough.'

Words die on the page.
Words die on the airwaves.
Fighters say that their words will win.
Mourners lament dead words.
Fighters compete with words
to say that their dead words deserve
more sorrow than other dead words.
The dead know nothing
of these dead words.

I met a man yesterday
who said he cooked himself a paella
and was ill for a fortnight.
He talked of lying on the floor
a pain in his stomach
like he had never felt before
and
everything going straight through him.
He stared ahead
full of the misery and mystery
of how a prawn
could make so much pain.

One way that we learn how
murderers show mercy
is when they point out that
they didn't kill all the people
they could have killed.

I sub-let my student flat to Howard Marks
in 1969.
He told me
the whole of life is in rock'n'roll.
He played me
The Name of the Place is I Like it Like That.
There you are, he said.
He slept on the floor
and played his records so loud
that he blew out my speaker.
Mr Nice.

I walked to where I am.
I'm too tired to walk back.
Sisyphus kept trying.
Good old Sisyphus.
I'm not Sisyphus.
I'm Michael.
The story of me walking to where I am
and being too tired to walk back is not
The Myth of Sisyphus.
It's
The Myth of Michael.

Will this war
stop people wanting to kill again?

I must wear glasses when I go shopping
I must wear glasses when I go shopping
I must wear glasses when I go shopping
I must wear glasses when I go shopping
(that way, I won't come home with cream cheese
instead of hummus)
I must wear glasses when I go shopping.

It's very nice
when people I haven't seen for a while,
tell me that they're glad
I'm alive.
I say,
It's better than being dead.

The train that I was going to catch
was cancelled
but the earlier train was so delayed
it arrived when the cancelled train was going to arrive.
One train turned into another train.
And you couldn't see how the trick was done.

You can't say that if you didn't say this.
This!
But you only said this because
I pointed out to you that you didn't say this.
But I said this before you asked me
to say this.
But you didn't say this as prominently
as you said that.
But you didn't say that, you only said this.

I have discovered this morning
that the reason we have children
is so that the older they get
the more likely it is
they make banana cake.

A man gets up off the sofa
and walks out the room.
He leaves the television on.
He doesn't come back.
There is no one to watch the television.
People on the television
are talking as if people are watching them
on the television
but in this room
they are not talking to anyone.

'I am merciful,' said the Anteater,
'I don't eat every single ant.'

My secondary school was big enough
for not all teachers to know all students.
Some sharp kids invented someone called
Furd from form 5C.
If any of us got into trouble
and they asked for our name,
we said, 'Furd, 5C.'
Furd 5C got a lot of detentions that year.

When the tiger was away
the jackals ate the tiger cubs.
The tiger started eating jackals.
Two ants argued about who was right
and who was wrong.
The tiger pointed out
that it didn't make any difference
what the ants said anyway.

Going through the tunnel on Eurostar
I can see fish.

Partrick Vallance diary: 'PM meeting – begins to argue for
letting it all rip. Saying yes there will be more casualties but so
be it "they have had a good innings," before saying: "DC says
Rishi thinks just let people die and that's okay"'.
Guardian Nov 20 2023)

Out of bedrooms and wards
long lines of the dead
walk towards you
asking you,
'Who were you to decide that
our innings was over?
Who gave you the umpire's white coat
and upraised finger?
Did you think we would never speak
from the graves you gave us?'

Jolly old Boris
he always made us smile!
Seems like he was killing us
all the while!

Patrick Vallance wrote in his diary that Johnson said of the Pandemic:
'Most people who die have reached their time anyway.'

His worldview was ready to pounce on us
as if our 'time' is logged in on a universal spreadsheet
which gave him the right to send us off to the morgue.

A Prime Minister who thinks
our lives are governed by a cricket score card
with the twist that the scores are worked out
before the players take to the field.
Who writes this score card and why.
And what's the point of doing anything
to prevent disease, poverty or war, anyway?'

We lose all our children.
All the things we did with them are gone.
We can't talk about these things
with the child that's gone.
We can't have new things
with the child that's gone,
but then we can't have 'gone things'
with any of our children
because they are gone.

My legs are in everyone's way.
They grew when I was fourteen
and I've never been able to
shrink them.

The wasp was asked why he ate ants.
He said it was because they're not insects.

It goes on
till the ambulances are full of dying doctors
till the ambulances' route to the hospital
is blocked by bodies
till the ambulance sirens are worn out
and cannot wail anymore
till the ambulances are full of tears
till the ambulances die
till the ambulances admit that it's their fault
till there are no more ambulances
it goes on

Though my dad achieved a lot in his life
I think the one thing that he was most proud of
was to burp the whole of the word 'Beelzebub'
in a single burp.

Nominative,
vocative,
accusative,
genitive,
dative,
ablative,
laxative.

'Can I recommend that we slow the news down?' said the King's tutor.

'How do we do that?' said the King, 'News is news. It just happens.'

'Not so, your Majesty. We'll only release the Bulletins when we want to.'

'Won't they write their own Bulletins?'

'We'll ban them.'

'I'm not a bigot, am I?' said the King.

'You pick and choose,' said the King's tutor.

'Mm?' said the King.

'You're very good at not being a bigot in some situations and then you're a bigot in others.

In fact, you're the bigot you pretend you're not.

Well done.'

'That was a foul,' said the King,
watching the annual football match,
'their man kicked our man.'
'Don't worry,' said the King's tutor,
'we will kick ten of theirs.'
'But the ref will send our men off and we'll lose,'
said the King.
'Not necessarily,' said the tutor.

The gardener has chopped down the forest, sir,' said the King's
tutor, 'the road can go through there now.'
'Good,' said the King, 'have the tree-lovers noticed?'
'Possibly,' said the tutor, 'but I've sent them to look at the Great
Tree on the Hill that was chopped down earlier.'

'Time to look at the penal code, sir,' said the King's tutor.
'Really?' said the King.
'Look: cursing the King – one year in prison,' said the tutor.
'And?' said the King.
'I suggest, the punishment for cursing the king should get the heaviest sentence of all,' said the tutor.

'Tell me that story, I like,' said the King.
'Once there was a man who wasn't there.
He was arrested and brought before the judge.
He was found guilty and sentenced to death.
He was executed. This story doesn't exist,'
said the King's tutor.
'I love that one,' said the King.

The fuse has blown.
See it. Say it. Shorted.

.

'What do the people like, facts or stories?'
said the King.
'Stories,' said the King's tutor.
'So if I want them to like what I'm doing,
tell them a story about it?'
'That's it, sir.'
'And if I don't want them to care about something,
just throw facts at them?'
'That's it, sir.'

Big compliment tonight at the signing.
A woman said that my book
was the only thing that stopped her baby
getting upset when she was doing its nappy.
Quote for the cover?
'This is a great nappy-changing book'.

I wonder
how many people who insist the Parthenon Marbles
should stay in UK have been to the museum and seen them?
how many would notice the difference
if replicas were made and put in the British Museum
in place of the originals?

News in:
A huge wooden horse has been found in the British Museum.
Sounds of armour clanking have been heard coming from
inside the horse.

As the King and the King's tutor rode across the battlefield, the
tutor shouted, 'I think we should stop doing this.'
'You're a traitor and a collaborator,' said the King.
They rode on some more.
'I think we should stop doing this,' said the King.
'Good idea, sir', said the tutor

there are times when a cold seems to advance across your face, up your nose, down your arms, across your back, you announce it to yourself, you go to bed, and in the morning it's gone, not there, slipped away in the dark, to find someone else

'After we've gone,' said the King,
'will people write history books about us?'
'Yes,' said the King's tutor.
'Good,' said the King.
'Don't get excited,' said the King's tutor,
'hardly anyone will read them.'
'But – but – that stuff where we... er...'
'Lied? It's the past. And once we're dead,
we can't be had for it.'

'What's that moving in the shed at the bottom of the palace garden?' said the King.
'Don't worry about that, sir,' said the King's tutor.
'Is it... people?' said the King.
'Really, sir, no need to worry about it.'
'But who are they? Do they talk?'
'Really sir, just ignore them.'

'The courts are full, sir, there's only time for one trial today,' said the King's tutor.
'Go on,' said the King.
'Either a General for killing some prisoners
or someone for shouting "Down with the King!"'/
'Try the villain who shouted 'Down with the King!', said the King.

'News from the Emperor, sir,' said the King's tutor.
'Yes?' said the King.
'He urges you to go easy on the prisoners,' s
aid the tutor.
'Should I take notice?' said the King.
'He has just supplied you with more thumbscrews,'
said the tutor.
'So that's a no, then,' said the King.

'The people are demanding you don't execute the prisoner,' said
the King's tutor.
'It must go ahead,' said the King,
'otherwise my enemies will say I'm lenient.'
'May I suggest, sir, that you cancel the execution
on the grounds that you're merciful?'
'Very good,' said the King.

'When I die,' said the King.
'I will be buried in a huge mausoleum.'
'Me too,' said the King's tutor.
'Not so,' said the King.
'Why's that?'
'As I'm more important than you,
my death is more important than yours,'
 said the King,
'so my grave will be bigger than yours.'

Are you a pessimist or an optometrist?

Just did my blood pressure.
It was $E = mc^2$.
(I think I'm doing it right. Is that good?)

'If God decides that I've done bad things,' said the King, 'I will
tell Him that that was because you told me to.'
'But all I did,' said the King's tutor, 'was say words. You did the
actions. '
'O well,' said the King, 'I'll say that what bad people said, made
me do bad things.'

'Do you think we'll get blamed?' said the King.
'How do you mean "we"?'
said the King's tutor.
'Me and you,' said the King.
'Slight mistake there, sir,' said the tutor,
'if by any faint chance we were summoned to explain things,
I would blame you and you would blame me.'

I need a mnemonic
to spell mnemonic.

'How does this football thing work?' said the King.
'When their side commits a foul, we all boo,'
said the King's tutor, 'and when our side commits a foul,
we shout, 'No foul!'
'What does the referee man do?' said the King.
'Doesn't matter. We just carry on,' said the tutor.

'Do you think I'm a great leader?' said the King.
'No sir,' said the King's tutor.
'Why's that?' said the King.
'You don't know what's going on
and you don't tell the truth,' said the King's tutor.
'Does that matter?' said the King.
'For the time being, no,' said the King's tutor

'Get rid of the dandelions in the garden,'
said the King to the King's tutor.
'Yes sir,' said the tutor,
'but this weedkiller will kill everything else.'
'Yes,' said the King, 'but that's alright I've hired Don Monty
to do a garden makeover. I'm thinking Versailles.'

'It's time for your ethics lesson,' said the King's tutor.
'We are good.'
'We are good,' said the King.
'So, if we are good, it's not possible for us to do bad things,' said
the tutor.
'So who then does bad things?' said the king.
'Bad people,' said the tutor.

'Time for your literature lesson now, sir,'
said the King's tutor, 'Macbeth.'
'O yes,' said the King, 'he was bad.'
'No,' said the tutor, 'he was good.'
'What!' said the King, 'Why?'
'Because he tried to fulfil his destiny,' said the tutor.

'I wish you wouldn't read *Where the Wild Things Are*
to your children, sir,' said the King's tutor.
'What!' said the King.
'It's terrible,' said the tutor,
'Max says he'll eat his mother.
A good book would have him going
to the land of the Wild Things and being eaten by them.'

'A fox has got in, sir and done terrible things to the chickens,'
said the King's tutor.
'What shall we do?' said the King.
'I'd recommend burning down the forest,'
said the King's tutor.
'What about the moles and rabbits and squirrels in there?'
said the King.
'I'd recommend burning down the forest,' said the King's tutor.

'The gardener says he's got rid of the hornet's nest,'
said the King.
'Please don't use those words,'
said the King's tutor.
'No?' said the King.
'Try 'Taken steps to deal with the problem',
said the tutor.
'Have we?' said the King.
'That's beside the point,' said the tutor

'We're doing very well, aren't we?' said the King.
'Shhh!' said the King's tutor.
'What's the matter?' said the King.
'You have to look as if things are tough for you,' said the tutor,
'that way people will sympathise with you. People don't like
winners.'

'Where are we?' said the King.
'On the moral high ground,'
said the King's tutor.
'How did we get here?' said the King.
'By saying we're more moral than everyone else,'
said the tutor.
'Are we?' said the King.
'Of course not,' said the tutor,
'but we say it the loudest.'

'Sir, you've hanged the wrong man,' said the King's tutor.
'O dear,' said the King, 'does that mean trouble?'
'No, sir,' said the tutor, 'just blame it on the hanged man.'
'But we hanged him,' said the King.
'No, sir, he shouldn't have been there, when we were knotting the rope.'

'You haven't done much subduing recently,' said the King's tutor.
'But I did some subduing to become King,' said the King.
'That's why you need to carry on subduing,' said the tutor.
'Carry on subduing. That sounds like it could be the title of something,' said the King.

'Psst, tutor, am I winning or losing this game of chess against William the Egghead?' said the King.

'Both, sir,' said the King's tutor.

'Both? How can it be both?' said the King.

'The only way you can win is to pretend you're losing, sir' said the tutor.

'What happens when this is over?' said the King.

'This,' said the King's tutor.

'You mean that this goes on and on?' said the King.

'Sure,' said the tutor.

'But I thought that once we've done this, there's no more this,' said the King.

'There's always more this,' said the tutor.

'Do the people love me?' said the King.
'Yes sir,' said the King's tutor.
'Does the world love me?' said the King.
'Yes sir.'
'Does God love me?' said the King.
'Yes, sir.'
'Do you love me?'
'No sir.'
'Why not?' said the King.
'I'm the only one to know you,' said the tutor.

'Are my people starving, tutor?' said the King.
'No sir,' said the King's tutor.
'Look through the window of our carriage: some people are eating feathers,' said the King.
'That is a problem,' said the tutor, 'they're doing that because they are stupid.'
'Fine,' said the King.

'Ow!' screamed the tutor.

'What?' said the King.

'I've got a splinter in my foot,' said the tutor.

'My doctor says that the best thing for a splinter in the foot is to amputate the leg,' said the King, 'shall I call for him?'

'Seems like the best thing to do,' said the tutor.

'I've got a report that says people are starving,' said the King.

'That's true,' said the King's tutor,

'but I think we should be very careful about what we call it.

"Starving" is offensive to those who starved last year.'

'"Thinning?' said the King.

'Much better,' said the tutor

'When I was at school,' said the King's tutor, 'we had a headteacher who caned the whole school.'

'Did no one say anything about it?' said the King.

'O yes,' said the tutor, 'the inspectors said after each caning that the headteacher should be very careful.'

'O, fair enough,' said the king.

The king of the foxes called the foxes together for a meeting.

'We need to do more to protect chickens,' he said.

'What a kind king,' the foxes said to each other.

'But, your majesty,' said one of the foxes, 'you said "do more to protect chickens". That sounds as if we are doing something to protect chickens at the moment. So I ask, "More than what?"'

'Good point,' said the King, 'but please take my goodwill as evidence that I mean well.'

'Yes,' said everyone, and they all went off on the usual night hunt for chickens.

'Do you like Shakespeare's *Richard III*, sir?'
said the King's tutor.
'No,' said the King.
'You should,' said the tutor, 'you have to see that all his bad deeds are motivated by the fact he's a victim of his physical state.'
'I don't get it,' said the King.

It's everything but it's nothing
it's all we've got but we've got nothing
we're on our own but we never are
we make of it what we will but we're made before
it happens now but only with what has happened
it's here now but then it's gone
we've got it now then we lose it

'What's the plan?' said the King.
'We'll turn the prison into a palace,'
said the King's tutor.
'And the prisoners?' said the King.
'There aren't any,' said the tutor.
'Oh, where are they?' said the King.
'Executed or transferred,' said the tutor.
'Well done,' said the King.

The poetry is unseen
it moves like the shadow in the night
like the hour hand of the clock
like the growth of the hair on your head
like the evaporation of the sea
like the frost on the car roof
like the arrival of sleep
like the word in the closed book

Chalk, they said,
is made of micro-fossils and nanno-fossils
so small we don't know they're there.
Living creatures petrified
made invisible to the human eye
but en masse and dead
they are useful.

'Sir,' said the King's tutor, 'I need to look over some of your old
letters, to write the history of your reign.'
'I don't know where they are,' said the King.
'Aren't they in your Letters Chest?' said the tutor.
'They got out,' said the King.
'What a pity,' said the tutor.

'When I'm beating my children,' said the King,
'what should I say to them?'
'Say that it's their fault,' said the tutor, 'you wouldn't be doing it,
if they hadn't been bad,' said the tutor
'But isn't it me doing the beating?' said the King
'What else could you do?' said the tutor.

'Sir,' said the King's tutor, 'Bluffbeard the Bard will trouble you
no more.'
'That's good,' said the King, 'he attacked me with his verses.'
'Do you know the line, 'I gave commands; then all smiles
stopped'?' said the tutor.
'No,' said the king
'I do and I did,' said the tutor

'When did history begin?' said the King.

'When we say it does,' said the tutor.

'So if I say history began yesterday, it began yesterday?' said the King.

'Yes,' said the tutor.

'But no one will believe me,' said the King.

'You're the King,' said the tutor, 'they'll believe you.'

'What is morality?' said the King.

'A code of behaviour universally applied,' said the King's tutor.

'Does it apply to us?' said the King.

'No,' said the tutor.

'It's not universal then,' said the King.

'No, but we say that it is,' said the tutor.

'I have one of your letters, but I can't open it,' said the tutor.
'I tried opening it, but it's stuck down with a glue so gluey that even the most skilled gluemeisters are unable to unglue it,' said the King.
'I could use a knife?' said the tutor.
'Don't you dare,' said the King.

'Horatio the Holy says the enemy will never be forgiven for their sins, sir,' said the King's tutor.
'That's good,' said the King, 'what about our sins? Will we be forgiven?'
'Horatio the Holy says we don't sin,
so we do not need to seek forgiveness.'
'Oh good,' said the King.

'Time for Maths, sir,' said the tutor.
'Your problem today, sir, is to work out the difference between
a) how long it will take a village to reproduce itself, if 90% of
the men leave and b) if 90% of the women and children leave.'
'What an absurd problem,' said the King.

'Was that our poison we sold the Prince?'
said the King.
'Yes,' said the King's tutor.
'I hope he hasn't poisoned anyone with it,'
said the King.
'We'll do our best to find out,' said the tutor.
'And if we have?' said the King.
'We'll condemn him, sir, and sell him some more.'

Comedians invented old age.
They scripted it so that we're parodies
of our younger selves,
trying to imitate the way we danced
or did our hair
and even waking us up every morning
with big plans and ambitions
like build a cathedral,
or go shopping.

*

Sir, the Royal hound has escaped,'
said the King's tutor.
'But I thought you taught it not to escape,'
said the King.
'Yes, but right now it's out in the woods. It's rampaging,'
said the tutor.
'I'll order it to come back,' said the King.
'Too late for that,' said the tutor.

'Two wrongs don't make a right. Correct?'
said the King.
'Correct, sir, except when you want people to think your wrong is right,'
said the King's tutor.
'But doesn't that make the first wrong, right?'
said the King.
'Yes,' said the tutor.
'Good,' said the King, 'so long as people don't tell us the two rights make a wrong.'

'We defeat evil by being good, don't we?'
said the King.
'Yes,' said the King's tutor, 'except when we defeat evil by being evil.'
'Won't that lead people to say we're evil?'
said the King
'Yes,' said the tutor, 'but we know we're good so they're wrong.'
'I see,' said the King.

I get an alert for a press article about me,
I click on it,
I have to scroll through 50 pictures
of big close-ups of warts and moles
(and how to get rid of them).
It's a new genre:
Wart Porn.

What's this?

succulent inside
golden and crusty outside
cut open- it steams

A pie-ku

'Are we doing something?'
said the King.
'O yes,' said the King's tutor.
'What?' said the King.
'We're talking to people behind the scenes,'
said the tutor.
'O that's good,' said the King, 'anything else?'
'No, not really,' said the tutor.
'I'll announce that then,' said the King.

'You'll see here, sir,' said the King's tutor, 'how the spider weaves
a web to catch flies.'
'Is that a good idea?' said the King.
'I'm not discussing that,' said the tutor, 'I'm describing it.'
'I think you're trying to justify it,' said the King.
'I'll continue,' said the tutor

As I shut my eyes
to go to sleep last night
a bouquet of dark roses
threatened me.
I tried to find out
if the roses
were in both eyes.
They were only on the right.

You've been putting the chocolate wrappers
back in the tin
so now you're not sure
if you've got any chocolates left.
You put your hand in
rummage about hoping
there is one last chocolate
but you keep finding
wrapper after wrapper after wrapper
but is that one a chocolate...?
Is it? Is it?

It's hard on ourselves
to say what our lost children
might have done.
It hurts.
I try to think
that he did what he did
in the time that he had.
He didn't own his future.
He owned his past
and his present.

My Dad used to say,
'Why do today what you can put off till tomorrow?'

One Christmas
my father (a secondary school English teacher)
waited till the end of term
went into the Art Room
gathered up the students' artwork
and brought it home.
That Christmas
our walls were covered with
15-year-olds' pictures of ghosts and dragons.

On the train this evening
I was kissed by a drunk Italian man called Paolo
who told the whole train
that his mother says he can do what he wants
but his wife tells him to be quiet.
She was sitting next to him
and told me that she was Brazilian.

At the theatre yesterday,
a woman with a stick and very bent over,
came up to me and said,
'I've got sciatica.
Old age is not for wimps.'

Hold in your eyes
the instant
when all round the table
we, who are spread
across eighty-three years of living,
linked by intricate threads,
looked at each other
and without knowing why
smiled.

Education invented the idea
that poems are egg-boxes
and what we do is take the eggs out
and when all the eggs are out
the poem is done.
But people have discovered that
you can boil eggs, or fry them,
or put some in a cake.
And you can juggle them too.

...when you drop a line to a doctor friend to say,
'Come over some time'
and they say, they'll be working in hospital right through
Christmas and the New Year....
(Please remember this,
Ministers and Shadow Ministers of Health)

Ban praline.
Abolish praline
No more praline
What do want?
Definitely not praline
When do we not want it?
Now and forever more.
Stop praline now.
Stop praline now.

The problem with trying to distract yourself
is that when you're trying to distract yourself
you keep noticing you're trying to distract yourself

Osmosis is how water gets into a bagel when it's being boiled.
Shmosmosis is how you know there are fresh bagels in the
room.
Osmosis shmosmosis is what you say when you can't answer
the osmosis question in a science exam.

We can't talk to dead people.
We can't hear their accounts
of their illness and death.
They're hidden in their medical notes.
Millions of stories not told.
Millions of stories not known.

Faint praise – unenthusiastic compliment
Feint praise – simulated compliment
Faint praise – compliment when not conscious

Here is a man
who shot and killed people
then burnt their corpses.
He goes home to his family
and tells them
it was a hard war.
He is arrested
tried
found guilty
put in prison
then released.
He lives a long and peaceful life.
He has regrets.
He regrets that while he was in prison
he couldn't see his grandchildren.

My belt,
led by the buckle
flips out of my hand onto the chair.
It rests
then dives to the floor,
wriggles
and rests again.
I put it on the chair
but it has other plans
and slides –
more slowly this time –
back to the floor
where it lies still.
Sleeping. Not dead.

Purple Rain – song
Purple Reign – glorious monarchy
Purple Rein – colourful horse gear

My hair (and beard) cut today
at the great Memphis salon in Muswell Hill
 took us into discussions on:
are Arsenal lacking a number nine?
Slavonic influence on Yiddish,
a broken pelvis (mine),
what people say when they start to take a sabbatical,
hot towels.

In loo – in toilet
in lieu – instead of
in Lou – Louis' abdominal problem

I see – I view
I.C. – integrated circuit
I, Sea – Neptune

Sorry to the families at the book festival
that I didn't get to see
because I missed the train
 in a dream I had last night.
I am sorry also
that I was sorry in the dream
that I didn't call you in the dream
to tell you I had missed the train
in the dream.

While I was watching *Poor Things*
I started thinking
it reminded me of *The Hunting of the Snark*
but as I started thinking about *The Hunting of the Snark*,
I realised that I couldn't remember that it was a Snark
they were hunting.
But then it wasn't a Snark.
It was a Boojum.

Her break – Adele's first hit
Her brake – part of Adele's car
Herb rake – Adele's gardening tool

I said, 'Hello.'
He said, 'Hello.'
I said, 'My name's Michael.'
He said, 'I know. I came here before. I worked in your house.'
I said, 'Did you?'
He said, 'Yes.'
I said, 'Sorry, I don't remember things from then.'
He said, 'That's OK.'

Write-off – broken car
Right off – mouldy cheese
Rite off – Guy Fawkes Night cancelled

A girl aged about three or four
was on the bus singing the alphabet song.
She ended it with 'zee'.
I leant over and said,
'Listen here, young lady. In this country,
we say 'zed'.
If people like you say 'zee',
society will fall apart
and it'll be hard to hang on to civilisation.'
I thought it was obvious
to anyone reading this
that I didn't say anything of the sort
but several people were outraged
and said it was very nasty of me
to have said it.

Grade 8 – excellent
Greyed 8 – old vests
Grey date – senior citizens' night out

Account – money in the bank
A Count – lesser nobility
A count – a misprint

Offspring reports that she was at the bus-stop
and there was a man with a boar's head under his arm.
The driver told the man
he couldn't get on the bus with a boar's head under his arm.
Back home I started to look up the regs
on carrying boar's heads on London buses.

Shit scared – very afraid.
Shits cared – unpleasant people were concerned

I came out of Oxford Circus Station
and a man said,
'You're either for Christ or anti Christ.
If you're not for Christ
you're anti Christ.
If you're anti Christ you're on the way to Hell.'
I said, 'I'm on the way to Pret for a sarnie.'

Relieve – create relief
Releave – springtime
Real eave – genuine part of a house

Yesterday
London Bridge Station
was full of empty notice-boards
and red 'X's marking each ticket barrier
as if we had made many mistakes
in our homework.
A cafe was open
optimistically.

Calling people a fruit cake
is beginning to worry me.
I resent the fruit-cake-ism
of using it as a slur.
What's to be done?

Grandchild stopped by a tree in the Ally Pally park.
The tree had one of those bulbous lumps sticking out of it.
She said it was a bum.
She said it was a Bum Tree.

We hunted for toys today.
Luckily there was a shop that does toys and haircuts.
The grandchild chose a DIY dentist kit.
Something for us all to look forward to.

On our walk today,
we went hunting for the Terrible Sausage.
It had escaped from a dinner.
We spotted a sign that said, 'Dead Hedge'.
We wondered if the Terrible Sausage
had killed the hedge.

I
had
a
chocolate
hob
nob.
Two
actually.
I had
two
chocolate
hob
nobs.
The
second
chocolate
hob
nob
was
as
good
as
the
first
chocolate
hob
nob.
If
not
better.

The NHS is in trouble:
under resourced.
Short of staff.
DIY tracheostomies are relatively simple.
Why not help the NHS
and give yourself a tracheostomy?

In times of armed conflict,
politicians know that it's good for them
if we argue over what things are called
and not over what is actually happening.
You'd have thought
that Shakespeare didn't ever write,
'A rose by any other name would smell as sweet...'

If we let children and older school students
have space to talk about
what they think of the books, plays, poems
they read in school,
they will get the chance to do
what those things were written for:
to help us understand ourselves.

Do children ever wonder why
it is that adults speak with such authority
about what children should do,
while at the same time wrecking the world?

That ad that says
millions of bacteria are hiding in your mouth....
er... they're not actually 'hiding', are they?
They're not hunkering down behind a tooth,
saying, 'They won't see us here.
Keep quiet and we'll be able to hang out here for days.'

Teachers know about teaching.
Writers know about writing.
Many teachers know about writing.
Some writers know about teaching.
When teachers and writers talk to each other,
good things happen.
Governments are not interested in these conversations.

I eat a lot of dried fruit.
Just sometimes a piece might have gone off
but you only find out when you're eating it.
Happened to me this morning.
Bad day.
Wrong date.

I once went to the doctor because I had a large spot on my leg.
He said, 'What do you think it is?'
I said, 'Cancer?'
He said, 'It's more serious than that.'
'Really?' I said.
'Yes, it's old age.'

'It's more serious than that' has become a catchphrase.

Street.
New Cross.
London.

Boy: Is it you?
Me: Yes.

The end.

Performing today at the New Wolsey Theatre
in front of a giant people-eating plant
because I was on the set of *The Little Shop of Horrors*.
I warned the children that either I or they
could be eaten.
Health and Safety precautions.

lunch was a starter of a small leftover of dal and rice
followed by an entrée of a small tranche of pizza
followed by a dessert of a quick bit of chopped herring on rye.
an indo-italo-Ashekenazi Jewish meal.

A builder came to the house.
I said, 'My name's Michael.'
He said, 'I know, I met you before
when I was decorating the living room.'
'You were here? In the house? When?'
'2019.'
'Ah I've forgotten 2019,' I said.

'...and there was a lovely party
for the 30th anniversary of *Bear Hunt*,' she said.
'Was there?' I said.
'Yes, you gave a speech.'
'Did I? When was this?'
'2019,' she said.
'Oh yes, I've forgotten 2019.'
'That's a shame,
there were lovely marzipan figures
of all the characters from the book.'

Friday night,
walking about with my son in Le Marais quarter of Paris.
Something about the cafés with the glassed-off eating areas at the
front, light pouring out on to the pavement.
People sitting talking.
People strolling across the square.
Apartments up above.

As I was coming out of the doctors
I met a woman
who had had a knuckle replacement.
She held up a bandaged hand
and said, 'It's the hand I draw with.
I'm an illustrator.'

I have a one-word answer for all Maths questions
on University Challenge:
'asymptote'.
I bark it out
(only in my brain so as to not annoy loved ones),
and it's never right.
But I might be getting nearer.
And nearer.

In this cafe
they've been playing the middle two verses
of Rod Stewart singing *I Don't Wanna Talk About it* –
over and over again,
for an hour.
Is the person running the cafe
trying to say something to someone?

When I switch off the TV
the pictures go away.
I can't see them.
I don't see them.
They are not there.
They are not in the room.
They are not with me.
The people who the cameras were pointing at
are not people anymore.
The people are not people.
They do not breathe or cry
or die.
I go into the kitchen.
I make myself some toast.

I've got a hole in my head
where memories were.
2 years of people, places and parties
left my head through the hole.
I didn't notice they were gone
until people said I was 'there'.
Someone said he was in our house.
When he's not looking,
I study him,
but he must have left too.

Electric drills and sanders speak.
They say, 'Me-e-e-e-e-e-e-e-e-e.'
If you don't notice them the first time,
they say,
'M-E-E-E-E-E-E-E-E-E-E-E-E-E-E.'

It's raining so much
I'm wearing my mac
indoors.

There's a philosopher called Michael Rosen.
Academia send me refs to 'Michael Rosen'.
I get notices of these by email.
I can always tell by the scholar's name
which ones will be for philosopher Michael Rosen.
Often a German name.
Today, it's an essay on 'The truth about truth'.

Today I realised that
when we're asleep
we're awake.
And when we're awake
we're asleep.

That instant
when you go to scratch your eyebrow
and you hit the edge of your glasses
and they fly through the air
as if you were trying to see if your glasses
were gliders
and an imagined teacher from 60 years ago
says, 'Rosen! Out!'

When you're sitting on the loo
in college
and the light goes out
and as there are no windows
there is no glimmer coming in from outside
so you wonder
if it's the light behind your eyes
in your brain
that's gone out
but today you are a magician
you move your arm
and the light comes back on.

I've been in a cafe.
They were serving soup
with grilled bread.
I was wondering if this was
toast.

I was busy being coached by the IHRA code
in why I would be antisemitic
if I was 'holding Jews collectively
responsible for actions of the state of Israel'
when the Chief Rabbi said:
'the Jewish people is showing incredible strength
at this trying time – none more so than our heroic soldiers.'
As a member of the 'Jewish people'
I didn't know which way to go with this.
Is the Chief Rabbi saying
that the 'Jewish people' have an army?
And is his praise of this army
'holding Jews collectively responsible'
for at least some of the 'actions of the state of Israel',
in particular those carried out by its 'heroic soldiers'?

But then I thought I had an army:
the British Army.
Now I've got two armies?
Is there something special about me
that I need two armies
when so many other people
get along with just one?

Next door they haven't bought a donkey.
One of them is practising the trombone.

Dai posts a video of a great pianist.
He's amazing, I say.
Yes, Dai says, I told you about him before
but perhaps that was in your Blank Period.
I have a name for it now.
Like Picasso's Blue Period.
My Blank Period.

In 2024
the words 'humanitarian aid'
became antisemitic.
Apparently.

I realised
when I was a boy
that if I wanted to be a man
I would need to talk a lot about arterial roads.
I would also have to call articulated lorries,
artics –
especially ones going along arterial roads.

I have a switch in my brain
which instantly forgets titles.
Someone says, 'Great new film,
it's called 'Sea Green Tentacles'.
I hear 'great new film'
and instantly forget 'Sea Green Tentacles'.

The packet of sultanas had to be finished.
That's not to say that it was in a state of being inevitably
or necessarily finished.
No.
It was simpler than that.
There was a packet of sultanas.
I had to finish them.
I had to finish them
because the sultanas made me finish them.

Today
I ate out for lunch.
The meal I wanted was not available
they said.
Then I went to catch a train.
The train was cancelled.
Later I went out to eat.
The meal I wanted was not available
they said.

I'm beginning to see a pattern.

What if
we aren't trying to get to the future
but instead
we're trying to get to whatever we think
or imagine
was the best of the past?

I have to remind myself to keep my eyes open.
It's not that I shut them
but if I don't remind myself
I discover that the world has gone grey.
I then connect my mind with my eyelids
and make the discovery that my eyelids
have drooped.
Or that I've drooped them.

That moment when a place you know
and walk through
and think is just 'that place'
in fact, has a name.
The tunnel I know
that I walk through
and thought was just
'y'know, that tunnel under the railway'
is in fact The Penstock Tunnel.
It'll never be the same again.

It was the last dark chocolate covered dried fig,
marking a time that stretched back
across days and weeks
to the first dark chocolate covered dried fig.
Thank you for
the dark chocolate covered dried figs.
They have lasted till today.

At my Ally Pally show yesterday
I praised the giant concrete bagel
that sits next to the playground.
I made a chant out of the alternative ways of naming it:
Bagel beigel.
Beigel bagel.
bagel bagel
beigel beigel.
You had to be there to appreciate the hole thing.
Anyway,
you say beigel
I say bagel
Let's call the hole thing off.

Offspring has bought a plastic brain.
It's red.
He says he may need a bigger one.

The inner lining of my glasses case has come loose.
The inner linings of both my glasses cases have come loose.
This tells me that inner linings of glasses cases have a tendency
to come loose.
However,
glasses cases without linings are still usable,
so life goes on.

When I saw *20,000 Leagues Under the Sea*
in the cinema
I was eight years old
and thought that the water
that flows over the submarine
in the fight scene with the squid,
would overflow into the cinema.

What are these DNA matches?
I've got safety matches
and those long matches for lighting the gas.
DNA matches?
OK, but whose DNA?

The new loo roll
that has no beginning.
The new loo roll
that promised so much
The new loo roll
so full of potential
The new loo roll
a library of useful pages
but
now finding me
hunting for the first sheet
with my fingertips
on and on and on
but no –
there is no beginning.

I'm a defective train magnet.
Whatever train I get on
either becomes defective
or there's a defective train ahead.
If inspectors want to know
where defective trains are
they should just follow me around.

My left big toenail
has its own way of doing things.
It makes for itself a creamy shell,
an extra layer
of something that once lived,
like the cover of the ancient book
my father gave me.

Important message in my email Inbox:
Are you the Michael Rosen who wrote
'Induced Pluripotent Stem Cell–Derived Cardiomyocytes'?

At the hospital eye clinic
for my six-month check-up.
I was thinking the psychology department
could be called the I clinic.